I0099018

Keep the CHANGE!

Experience Lasting Life Change

Tom Zimmerman

Life Changers Press

Keep the Change! Experience Lasting Life Change

3rd Edition.

Requests for information should be addressed to:
Life Changers Press
P.O. Box 13322
Scottsdale, AZ 85267-3322

Library of Congress Cataloging-in-Publication Data

Zimmerman, Tom
Keep the Change! Experience Lasting Life Change / Tom Zimmerman.
p. cm.
ISBN-13: 978-0615468815
1. Self-actualization (Psychology) —Religious aspects—Christianity.
2. Success—Religious aspects—Christianity. 1. Title.

In the interests of privacy, some names have been changed.

Printed in the United States of America

This book is dedicated to:

The Holy Spirit,

enables me to change;

∞

Barbara, my wife and best friend,

helps me to change.

∞

In Him we live and move [and change]

and have our being. – Acts 17:28

Special Thanks

Over the years, I have enjoyed the amazing generosity and assistance of hundreds of different people. They have listened to me, counseled me, prayed for me, provided resources and even laughed at my jokes. My warmest thanks go to every one of you.

Many of the lessons I have learned in life have come in the context of family life. Thank you, my family, for sharing life and love with me.

In the five years since this book was first published, many friends and clients have read it and offered valuable feedback. I've tried to incorporate many of your comments and suggestions. Thank you.

Luke 6:38 tells us, "Give and it will be given to you." May you be blessed as generously as you blessed me.

Table of Contents

How to Use this Book

This book may be different than you are accustomed to. It is intended to be part workbook, part inspirational, part motivational and, above all, challenging and practical. If I may I offer a few suggestions:

1. Write in this book. I've left plenty of room for you to jot notes, thoughts and questions, as well as to respond to the exercises.

2. Read each chapter twice, then complete the assignments before going on. Take your time to work through the book. Ideally, work through one chapter per week.

3. Do the Life-Changer assignment at the end of each chapter.

4. Use the FOCUS pages to stimulate your relationship with God. You'll find one at the end of each chapter. At the bottom of each FOCUS page are additional Bible passages to study, one for each day of the week.

5. Share what you learn with others. It will bless them and help you to understand more deeply.

6. Read. Reflect. Pray. Do.
The ultimate goal is life change, so don't forget to apply what you learn.

About the Author

Dr. Tom Zimmerman has been a pastor, missionary and campus worker. For the past 19 years, he has directed Life Changers Counseling. Tom and Barbara have been married 34 years, have 2 adult children, 1 grandchild and live in Arizona, where they enjoy camping, hiking and sailing.

To learn more about the. author and Life Changers, or if you would like to share your story how *Keep the Change!* has helped you, please see the Life Changers website: www.azchristiancounseling.com.

Introduction

Welcome to the Book that almost refused to be written! Fifteen years ago I began writing down thoughts about life change. After all, that is a big part of my profession. I direct a Christian counseling service called Life Changers Counseling. I help people grow and change every day.

However, life change is more than just a profession for me. It is a passion. I long to be transformed into what I can become, because the results are so much greater than what I am right now.

In the same way, I find it extremely gratifying when others catch the vision of life change and experience it for themselves. So, a book about life change should be a no-brainer.

Why, then, did it take 15 years? Naturally other things got in the way: kids in college, a busy counseling ministry, 9/11, the economy…as well as the "bunny trails" I allowed to distract me. I think, though, the past 15 years have helped me gain a valuable perspective about how we change, or, really, how God helps us to grow and change.

I've divided the book into three sections:

Part 1: Understanding the Life Change Process

Here, we will consider the how's and why's of life change.

Part 2: Overcoming the Hurdles to Change

We then identify and confront the obstacles that keep us from changing.

Part 3: Building a Strong Foundation for Change

Finally, we look at the key building blocks for changing your life.

In each section, I've tried to strike a good balance between the philosophical, the theological and the practical. I trust you will profit from the time we spend together on these pages.

Part 1

Understanding the Life Change Process

1 Welcoming the Winds of Change

The wind is all around us. It constantly brings something new: new breaths of air, leaves, particles of dust, butterflies...they all come from somewhere else and change our environment.

> *The only person who likes change is a baby with a wet diaper! - Mark Twain*

Sometimes, we delight in the wind, enjoying its soft fingers on our skin. Often, we ignore the refreshing breezes that change our environment. We take the wind for granted and forget its impact on our lives. We can resist the wind and resent the changes it brings. We try to maintain the status quo, but the wind still keeps coming. Change is inevitable.

We Resist Change

One of the basic principles taught in management classes is that people resist change. We don't like to change in our organizations and we don't like change in our personal lives. Yet, change is one of those things we all know we need. Why are we so hesitant to allow it to happen to us?

We resist change because it involves taking away the accustomed and the familiar, replacing it with something we might not like, something foreign and unfamiliar. Of course, we usually don't get too worked up over changes that don't really affect us. If they raise the price of broccoli at the grocery store, it may not bother someone who never buys broccoli.

In the same way, we get accustomed to certain changes that happen in society. When the automakers change the look of their models for the coming year, it doesn't bother most of us all that much. We are used to the idea that styles of cars and dresses and music will gradually change from year to year. As consumers, we have the choice whether to buy into these changes, or not. We choose whether to adjust our shopping habits, based on our personal preferences.

> *We don't like change, because we fear it will make things worse.*

There are other changes, though, that we really don't like. When change is imposed on us from the outside and it affects us personally, we become more resistant. Whether it involves a change in the homeowners' association rules, a change in speed limits or a change in the vacation policy at work, we are easily irritated at the disruption. We especially resent changes that are forced upon us, things over which we have little influence. Most of us have learned to passionately resist such uncomfortable impositions.

Exercise 1

Think with me for a moment. What changes can you think of that were imposed on you by someone else? What didn't you like about them? Take a moment and write them down here:

Why We Don't Like Change

For many of us, we object more to the way changes are presented than we object to the changes themselves. In essence, we don't really like others telling us what to do, what to believe, how to act or what to think. This isn't really surprising. I don't know of too many thinking people who like to be ordered around! Here is something important for us to recognize:

Others have imposed changes on us and we definitely don't like the bad taste it left in our mouths.

Another factor to consider is:

We think we don't like change, because too often we have had a bad experience with change.

You may not like to call it fear, but whether you call it fear, anxiety, apprehension, concern…it is the same thing. We fear something new not only because we have had bad experiences in the past, but because changing things brings more uncertainty about the future. It is part of our nature to want to control our world, to keep things as they are, to not let those changes happen, because we believe they will be changes for the worse.

What if you could experience a different type of change?

What if certain changes weren't forced on you, but instead were things you recognized as valuable and important for your life? What if no one was requiring you to change, but you personally chose it? What if you were motivated to risk leaving the old familiar patterns for a new way of approaching life? And, what if you could let go of some of your fears, because you knew God is right there with you in the change process and He hasn't forgotten about what you need. What if you trusted Him to help you change, that your life would significantly improve?

Would you still object to change?

Can We Change?

Another reason people resist changing their lives is they don't believe it will work. They have already tried to change in the past and have been largely unsuccessful.

Everyone has either dieted unsuccessfully or knows someone who has faced this frustration. Even if, in the short-term, someone loses 10 or 15 pounds, many inevitably put the weight back on within months. Indeed, we all have conquered bad habits, only to fall prey to them again in a time of weakness. From experiences like these, we have invariably learned that changes don't last. We have come to believe change is bad, it may hurt and, ultimately, we can't really change anyway.

Is it True?

Is it really true that we can't change? Even if your experiences have told you so, does it mean you are forever destined to remain as you currently are?

Jody was a young mom who was at the end of her rope. Her husband suddenly left home, claiming she was no longer good enough for him. Jody was depressed and feared life as a single mom. She came to believe she was worthless, destined to fail at life.

But she didn't fail. With help from her church, Jody got back in touch with God. One step at a time, one day at a time, Jody began to change. She discovered God still loved her and others still believed in her. She even started to believe in herself and in the abilities God had given her.

As she experienced God's love and kindness, Jody became more effective in loving her kids. She found a job and learned to provide for her family. Over several months, Jody gained a totally new perspective on life. She could smile and look forward to the future once again.

I hope you'd agree with me there are countless stories of people who have indeed changed their lives significantly. They quit old habits, got better, became more productive, more loving, more committed. The Bible and modern history are full of people who found a way to overcome themselves and their circumstances.

> *People who successfully change and develop their lives over the long-haul are people who are personally motivated and willing to try a totally new approach to their problems.*

What did they have that allowed them to experience lasting, positive change, while so many other people wallow in the same old issues their whole lives? How did they "keep the change?" How did they make life change last?

The answer is very simple. I don't mean this is a simplistic approach, but it is very simple, or straight-forward.

They have learned that pounding their heads against the same wall isn't the answer, even if it's in a different spot! Instead, they used a new approach to getting past the wall that is holding them back from reaching their dreams.

Have you ever been in a situation where you are getting nowhere? You've hit the wall and bounced back time and again. Maybe you are dealing with something like that right now.

Exercise 2

What is holding you back in life? Take a moment and write it down:

If you found something to write down, you're in good company. I don't know anyone who doesn't need to grow past something in their lives.

Don't we all have issues and challenges? Even when everything looks great on the outside, it often isn't really that way.

The Supernatural Power to Change

As we consider change, one hindrance keeps coming up: ourselves. We limit our own ability to change. By the very fact that we are human and fallible, we naturally hold ourselves back from becoming what we can and should become. So, why should it be any different this time?

> *The good news is we don't have to go it alone. It has actually been God's plan all along to transform us into the better "us."*

I'm certainly going to teach you some new ways to look at your past, present and future life. I'm also going to motivate you to change and teach you skills to help bring about life change; but, if we don't have the supernatural power of the One who made us and knows us completely, we will fail miserably at every attempt to change.

In our journey in the coming chapters, I hope you'll come to welcome His help and trust Him in the important work of rebuilding.

At the beginning of this chapter I wrote about the winds of change. Would you do something with me right now? Use your imagination to envision gentle winds all about you. These breezes are bringing change and opportunity to your life. They are bringing something new, different from your regular routine. They are offering you God's message of freedom from your past mistakes and the present life patterns that hold you down.

Now, lift up your face and welcome the winds of change.

Life-Changer #1

Each week as you proceed through *Keep the Change!*, I'll give you different assignments. It is important that you complete each of the activities (don't just read them and go on!). Over the coming week, I'd like you to do the following:

1. Re-read this chapter at least once and prayerfully review these thoughts frequently. Ask yourself what you need to learn and change. Ask God to give you a willing attitude and perseverance in the weeks ahead.

2. FOCUS daily. To aid the change process, please take 10 minutes each day of reading, reflection and prayer. It is best that you FOCUS at the beginning of each day. Please use the FOCUS worksheets provided at the end of each chapter to get you started. Begin with reading the Scripture passage, then reflect on and write out your challenge, focus and prayer for today. Conclude your FOCUS time with prayer about these things.

That's it for now! Don't worry, there will be plenty more in the chapters to come.

Focus — Read. Reflect. Pray. Do.

Psalm 1:1-6

Blessed is the man who does not walk in the counsel of the wicked or stand in the way of sinners or sit in the seat of mockers. But his delight is in the law of the LORD, and on his law he meditates day and night.

He is like a tree planted by streams of water, which yields its fruit in season and whose leaf does not wither. Whatever he does prospers.

Not so the wicked! They are like chaff that the wind blows away.

Therefore the wicked will not stand in the judgment, nor sinners in the assembly of the righteous. For the LORD watches over the way of the righteous, but the way of the wicked will perish.

What is the main point of the passage?

How does it apply to me?

My Challenge Today

What challenges / opportunities await me today?

How do I want to respond to them?

My Focus Today

What is my guiding thought for today?

My Prayer Today

Specific things I am trusting God for:

For Further Study this Week

John 1:1-18, John 1:19-50, John 2:1-11, John 2:12-25. John 3:1-21, John 3:22-36

2 Change We Can Really Believe In

In 2008, Barack Obama ran for president on the slogan "Change you can believe in." This campaign theme energized millions of voters who were dissatisfied with the direction of the nation and with their personal lives. People began to hope that things would really change.

> *Therefore if anyone is in Christ, he is a new creature; the old things passed away; behold, new things have come.*
> *– Paul, 2 Corinthians 5:17*

As I write this, in 2016, some of the promised changes have come and many others are on the horizon, but people are still dissatisfied and more disillusioned than ever. A major backlash developed across the nation, in the form of the Tea Party movement. It seems the changes have been too abrupt for many (head-over-heels change), while not enough for others (incremental change).

While I fully support being active in the political process, I believe whatever political changes are enacted still fall in the external changes I discussed in the first chapter. Ultimately, they don't satisfy our needs or longings for lasting change.

The Need for Lasting Change

Just yesterday I met Marsha, a glamorous young woman who appears to have it all together: friends, health, wealth and a beautiful appearance millions of other women "would die for." As Marsha told me her story and the tears from her deep pain began to flow, it reminded me once again that we are all in the same boat. There is something in life trying to hold back each one of us. Each of us needs to grow. None of us can always do it right. None of us can do it alone.

This brings us back to the idea of fundamentally changing your approach to life. This new approach focuses not on changing the outside: your circumstances, your money, your schedule... because even if you could change the outside, it really doesn't bring the joy and peace in life that you long for. Instead, you need to focus on change beginning from the inside and letting this work to the outside. You need to *Keep the Change!*

As you begin to change on the inside, you'll learn to have a better, more accurate perspective of who you are and what you have to offer to your world. You will become more fulfilled and more at peace as you allow this change process to radiate out through you to those God brings into your life.

> *As you work through* ***Keep the Change!****, you will learn to develop lasting, meaningful change, which will affect the quality of your life, your relationships and your future.*

Now that we understand the change process needs to start on the inside, let's begin to look at how things are inside: how we view ourselves.

How we think about ourselves is crucial to our personal success. What you do and how you live is based in large part on what you believe about yourself: Am I valued? Am I important? Am I okay? Am I capable? Do my self-doubts overwhelm my optimism?

Let's develop this a little further. In Exercise 3, you can begin this self-inventory process.

Exercise 3

Take a few moments and list your thoughts to these questions:

Am I valued? By whom?

Am I important? To whom?

Am I okay?

Am I capable?

Now write about your doubts and misgivings:

How do I doubt myself?

What am I uncertain about?

What do I fear?

Bobby was a young man in my campus ministry who was filled with uncertainty. He was afraid to even order a meal at the restaurant, fearful he would choose the wrong thing. His domineering mother had repeatedly warned him about making mistakes in life, to the point where he was unable to make any decisions on his own.

One of his friends, Stephen, was totally different. Although he also had some baggage from his family, Stephen had a confident, optimistic outlook on life. He not only was secure in His relationship with God, he also had confidence in his own abilities and in God's working in his life.

A person filled with doubts about his self-worth will be greatly limited in his personal life development and less capable of love and service to society. In contrast, a person who is convinced of his value and abilities will be more aware of his personal needs and better prepared to succeed in life. We find this truth in the Book of Proverbs:

For as he thinks within himself, so he is. — Solomon, Proverbs 23:7

The essence of successful living, then, is how you perceive yourself and how you build on that perception.

One of our biggest challenges is to get away from "stinking thinking" and embrace healthy thinking, which leads to healthy self-esteem and healthy behaviors.

Paul expanded on this in his letter to the church in Ephesus:

> *...put off your old self, which is being corrupted by its deceitful desires; to be made new in the attitude of your minds; and to put on the new self, created to be like God in true righteousness and holiness. — Paul, Ephesians 4:22-24*

Imagine a homeless person who is invited to enter a caring shelter where he can take off and discard his old rags, wash himself thoroughly and put on brand-new clothing just his size. He is welcomed and accepted, safe and not judged by his mistakes. He is renewed. Imagine how good that must feel.

With God's help, we can get rid of wrong thinking and behaviors, be renewed and refreshed and put on a new godly life where we feel good about ourselves. Imagine how wonderful it will be to experience the lasting change God has in store for you.

As you develop in your view of yourself and learn to practice this in everyday life, you will rapidly progress to becoming the man or woman you want to be and were intended to become. You will *Keep the Change!*, changing from the inside-out to experience the joy and blessing of a successful, healthy life.

Life-Changer #2

1. Re-read this chapter at least once and summarize what you have learned:

2. FOCUS daily. To aid the change process, please take 10 minutes each day of reading, reflection and prayer. It is best that you FOCUS at the beginning of each day. Please use the FOCUS worksheets provided. Begin with reading the Scripture, then reflect on and write out your challenge, focus and prayer for today. Conclude your FOCUS time with prayer about these things.

FOCUS — Read. Reflect. Pray. Do.

Psalm 8:3-9

When I consider Your heavens, the work of Your fingers, the moon and the stars, which you have set in place,what is man that You are mindful of him, the son of man that You care for him? You made him a little lower than the heavenly beings and crowned him with glory and honor. You made him ruler over the works of your hands; You put everything under his feet: all flocks and herds, and the beasts of the field, the birds of the air, and the fish of the sea, all that swim the paths of the seas. O LORD, our Lord, how majestic is Your name in all the earth!

What is the main point of the passage?

How does it apply to me?

My Challenge Today

What challenges / opportunities await me today?

How do I want to respond to them?

My Focus Today

What is my guiding thought for today?

My Prayer Today

Specific things I am trusting God for:

For Further Study this Week

Proverbs 3:5-6, Eph. 4:22-24, John 4:1-26, John 4:27-54, John 5:1-15. John 5:16-47

3 The *Keep the Change!* Process

One of the things I most enjoy is sailing. I like sitting on our boat with friends. I like the splash of the water. I even like the odd jobs of cleaning and maintaining the boat. But, most of all, I like the thrill of cutting through the water as the power of the wind is harnessed and directed properly.

As we all know, wind can be a very destructive force. I have seen sailboats literally torn apart by the wind. On the other hand, when the wind is focused on the sail at the correct angle, the boat comes to life and sails away.

The difference between destruction and great sailing is a matter of focus. When our lives are unfocused and in disarray, we go nowhere. We easily fall into destructive life patterns. Yet, when we are focused, living with the right perspective and zeroing in on the right priorities, we move ahead in life.

Inside-Out Life

In Chapters 1-2, you learned of our need to change and how this change must be from the inside-out. Now, let's focus in on a few foundational concepts we need to grasp. They are key components of the life change process.

To get started, I'd like to introduce you to a few terms and ideas. Don't get scared off by the terms, they are just words to help us understand some basic concepts.

The first word we need to learn is a Greek word, *imago*. *Imago* refers to image, how we think of ourselves. For example, if you think of yourself as being pretty confident in life, this is part of your *imago*.

Everyone makes basic assumptions about themselves: who you are, what you are like, what you are good at, what you aren't so good at. Would you agree that you may be more critical of yourself than you should be? You may be much harder on yourself than God is. And, some of your assumptions are right, some are not.

That's why I call this your *assumed imago*. Your *assumed imago* is partly accurate and partly out-of-touch with reality. The *assumed imago* can actually be a lie, leading you to a wrong assumption about yourself.

> *... your assumed imago is what you believe about yourself; it dictates how you relate to yourself and to those around you.*

Let's think about the importance of this. Keith was a young man I counseled who had often been told by his father that he was small and weak and couldn't accomplish much. Even after Keith became a normal-sized man, he still viewed himself as a small, ineffective person of little significance. He had bought into a lie, or at best, a half-truth which led him to low self-esteem. He ultimately became morose because he believed he would never be a real man.

Do you see how our *assumed imago* can greatly impact our lives?

There is another *imago* we need to deal with, the *ideal imago.* The *ideal imago* is where you really want to be in life. It is who you were intended by God to be, what you were created to be.

Your *ideal imago* incorporates your dreams and values and longings for significance. It is the best you. It is your goal, what you should strive for. Your *ideal imago* is what you can and should become. When you reach for your *ideal imago*, you are reaching for a life of hope, peace, service and a sense of completeness.

The problem we as people face is that our *assumed imago* often doesn't allow us to get to the *ideal imago.* It gets in the way. Our wrong assumptions about ourselves lead us to wrong values and wrong habits which lead us in the wrong direction. That is what Keith did, by assuming he was weak and ineffective, which then limited his ability to grow and reach his ideal.

This conflict between the assumed and the ideal is the *imago crisis*, the breakdown between current reality and the dream for success and wholeness. Too often, this is where we give up.

Have you ever said, "I can't do it…it's too hard." Most of us have felt that way. The *imago crisis* comes when you hit the wall and seem to get no further in life. No amount of tweaking or pounding your head against the wall will ever get you to where you want to be, to where you need to be. Until you correct your assumptions and get a healthy view of yourself, you'll continue to be frustrated.

The beauty of changing your life from the inside-out is that there is no need for endless frustration and despair. You can do this, like thousands of others already have.

With God's help and by learning to apply some important principles, you will be able to:

- feel good about yourself.
- know that your life is back on track.
- grow toward your ideal imago.

Now that we've looked at these *imago* principles, I'd like you to begin to review your life assumptions and experiences. Please use the Life-Changer assignment below as your guide. As you work through the questions, prayerfully reflect on the things you believe about yourself. Look for the wrong conclusions or lies you have come to accept.

Life-Changer #3

This chapter's Life-Changer is more extensive. Don't worry; it will be well worth your time as you work through it.

Who I am versus who I have been told I am

1. What messages have you received from other people about yourself? Write down who has told you what about yourself?

2. The results of those messages: How have those messages affected you? What have you believed about yourself? This is your *assumed imago.*

3. What you have been told and what you believed about yourself isn't necessarily true. God's Word tells us the truth about ourselves. Study the following scriptures and summarize what God tells you about you.

   For You created my inmost being; You knit me together in my mother's womb. I praise You because I am fearfully and wonderfully made; Your works are wonderful, I know that full well.(Psalm 139:13-14)

   I am ______________________________.

For God so loved the world that He gave his one and only Son, that whoever believes in Him shall not perish but have eternal life. (John 3:16)

God ____________________________.

Since you are precious and honored in my sight, and because I love you, I will give men in exchange for you, and people in exchange for your life. (Isaiah 43:4)

I am ____________________________ to God..

So do not fear, for I am with you; do not be dismayed, for I am your God. I will strengthen you and help you; I will uphold you with my righteous right hand (Isaiah 41:10)

As I was with Moses, so I will be with you; I will never leave you nor forsake you.... Be strong and courageous. Do not be terrified; do not be discouraged, for the LORD your God will be with you wherever you go. (Joshua 1:5,9)

I am never____________________________.

God is ____________________________.

For it is by grace you have been saved, through faith—and this not from yourselves, it is the gift of God— not by works, so that no one can boast. For we are God's workmanship, created in Christ Jesus to do good works, which God prepared in advance for us to do. (Ephesians 2:8-10)

I don't have to earn God's ____________________________ .

He accepts me because of ____________________________ .

4. Summarize the truth God tells you about you. This truth is your *actual imago*:

5. Now, compare what you have believed about yourself and the truth of who you really are:

What I have believed	What is really true

6. The difference between what you believed about yourself and the truth about you is your *imago crisis.* This is where you need to focus: rejecting the old messages and embracing the truth about yourself.

   List the top three truths about yourself you need to embrace:

7. Now, talk to God about this person you just wrote about. You may want to write out your prayers in a journal. It sometimes helps them seem more real. As you pray, share your heart with the Father. Since He knows it already, you don't have to hold anything back. You can trust Him. Tell Him of your joys and your sorrows. Talk to Him about your feelings of insecurity, anger, pain, or other emotions.

After you have shared your feelings, ask God to help you. Ask Him for wisdom and insight. Ask Him to direct your thoughts. Ask Him to use this *Keep the Change!* Process so that you can become all He wants you to become.

8. Finally, thank God. No, you don't have to thank Him for your wrong mistakes or for the pain others caused you. Thank Him for your future and the opportunity you have right now to change, with His help. Most of all, thank Him that He knows you better than you know yourself and He promises to be right beside you as you grow. He said, "I will never leave you nor forsake you." (Joshua 1:5)

9. Remember to continue with your daily FOCUS times as well.

Focus — Read. Reflect. Pray. Do.

Psalm 18:2-3

> *The LORD is my rock, my fortress and my deliverer; my God is my rock, in whom I take refuge. He is my shield and the horn of my salvation, my stronghold.*
> *I call to the LORD, who is worthy of praise, and I am saved from my enemies.*

What is the main point of the passage?

How does it apply to me?

My Challenge Today

What challenges / opportunities await me today?

How do I want to respond to them?

My Focus Today

What is my guiding thought for today?

My Prayer Today

Specific things I am trusting God for:

For Further Study this Week

Isaiah 43:4, Isaiah 41:10, Joshua 1:5-9, Eph. 2:1-10, John 6:1-15
John 6:16-24

Part 2

Overcoming the Hurdles to Change

4 Running the Roadblocks

So far, we have looked at the basic idea of changing your life from the inside out. I introduced you to the inside-out concept, which is based on how you think about yourself and the assumptions you make. You also looked at how your *assumed imago* has influenced your past. As you develop your *ideal imago*, you'll find the freedom to become the person you're meant to become. In order to get there, there are a few things we need to overcome on the way.

> *I know quite certainly that I myself have no special talent; curiosity, obsession and dogged endurance, combined with self-criticism have brought me to my ideas.*
>
> \- Albert Einstein

The Roadblock

Some time ago, I saw a few minutes of the old movie, *Smokey and the Bandit*, on late-night television. Burt Reynolds played a wiley, hot-rodding street racer who always was able to outfox the local police trying to catch him. Most of the movie was a series of chase scenes which ended with the Bandit finding a way around the police roadblocks intended to stop him.

Sometimes I feel like the Bandit. I just want to get around the roadblocks of life, the things preventing me from the life I long for. The temptation to bypass the blockade with some trick or quick-fix approach is great.

Each of us runs into roadblocks where we are held back from what we so desire to attain. We know we need to get past them if we are ever to experience the life we were intended to live. So we ask, how can we overcome the roadblocks legitimately?

Look back at your work from last chapter. Do you remember the messages that have led you to your *assumed imago,* blocking you from your *ideal imago*? You have your specific *imago crisis*, roadblocks keeping you from where you want to and need to go.

Sometimes, these roadblocks are because of the messages from others and our reactions to them. I hope you are on your way to confronting those wrong messages and embracing truthful messages about how God sees you and has created you. Remember to keep repeating the truth and confronting the lies. This is a good start to running the roadblocks.

There are other roadblocks we face, too. Each of us has made wrong choices and decisions, making a mess of things. Sometimes, painful things have happened to us or we have been treated poorly by others.

We aren't at all happy with these situations, choices and messages, but these things have marked us in a deep and lasting way. We no longer view ourselves as we did before. Often, we just fall into a certain way of thinking about ourselves. These choices and situations also feed into that old *assumed imago*, resulting in a sense of low self-esteem.

Two years ago, I met Dave, a man in his 30's who was ready for a change in life. By the time we met, Dave had already tried a variety of things to make life better. He had developed an exciting career, but wasn't satisfied with his success. He married the woman of his dreams, yet ended up with the heartache of a broken relationship. Dave even bought a series of motivational tapes from a well-known speaker, but it seemed no amount of tweaking his life circumstances could bring him the joy and contentment he longed for.

Over a period of years, Dave gradually developed the assumption that he was woefully inadequate. He felt certain he was inadequate in love, in his career and as a man. How sad that anyone ever has to feel this way about himself!

But, here is the real kicker. Once Dave arrived at this negative view of himself, no level of achievement was great enough to quell his feelings of self-doubt and inadequacy. It was impossible to prove to himself that he was okay at anything. He was miserable, depressed and easily agitated. He had hit the wall and he couldn't seem to get past it. Dave had reached his *imago crisis*.

As I share Dave's story with you, maybe you can identify with him a little. Each of us faces those feelings of insecurity and uncertainty, where we feel the need to prove to ourselves and to others that we really are okay

It boils down to how we measure our sense of self-esteem. Think of self-esteem as a thermometer. Just like the red liquid goes up when it gets hot and goes down when it is cold, so also our self-esteem goes up and down.

We measure our self-esteem in a variety of ways: the subtle pressure to earn lots of money; the need to have the most talented, most well-behaved children; outward appearance; popularity in school, at work or at church; impressing the neighbors or the pastor or the boss or the spouse or the in-laws or yourself!

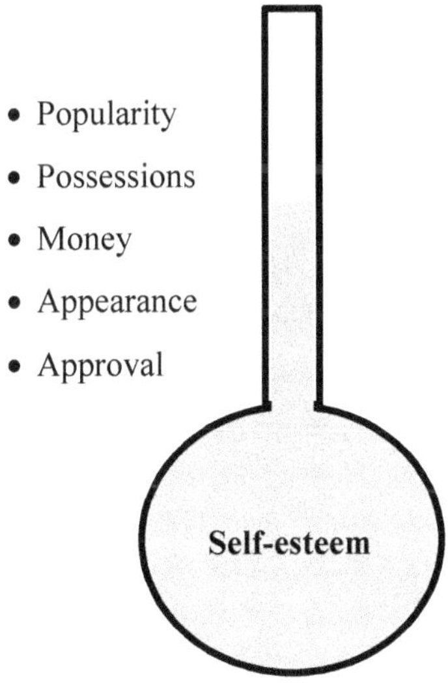

Exercise 4: How I measure my Self-esteem

I feel best about myself when I…

How do I prove (to myself or others) that I'm okay?

How do I try to prove it to God?

Even in the midst of proving yourself, if you are really honest with yourself, perhaps you'll agree there must be another way. You shouldn't have to perform. You shouldn't have to prove yourself to anyone, including yourself!

Running the Roadblock

Like Dave, most of us feel driven to perform for or to impress others, even if we know we shouldn't be under that pressure. But, we still feel inadequate, driven to perform and feel like we are getting nowhere in life.

Many of the things we use to measure our self-esteem are external. We rely on others to approve of us, accept us or validate us in some way. If we get that sense of approval, acceptance or validation from others, we feel okay for a while. It makes us dependent on the actions of others. We literally lock into a belief system where our sense of happiness and security hangs on what others may think about us!

In spite of these feelings, you need to remember:

God didn't create you to buy into a system of self-doubt and insecurity.

Instead of frustration and despair, He wants you to be free for a life filled with purpose, service and hope…a life of meaningful relationships…a life that reflects His love for you. But, how do you get there? How are you to respond to the challenges that hold you back so that you can move forward?

> *Whom have I in heaven but you? And, besides you, I desire nothing. My flesh and my heart may fail, but God is my strength and my portion forever. Psalm 73:25-26*

Start with God's truth. Psalm 73 describes a man who dealt with insecurity. He compared himself with others, ending up feeling inferior. He became despondent (v.21-22). Finally, though, he discovered the truth, that he didn't need people to approve of him, he just needed God.

Back to Dave's story…although his self-esteem was in the gutter, he reached out for God's help and began a beautiful healing process. He came to see that he had become dependent on others to affirm him, forcing him to perform for them. Dave overcame his roadblock by coming to accept that God loves him just the way he is. He was free to just be himself and to become the very best Dave he could become, not to prove himself, but because he wanted to grow!

The essential question is:

What will you do to confront and overcome your roadblocks so you can move on with your life?

Life-Changer #4

1. Your challenge is to confront your issues and overcome the roadblock of low self-esteem. As you consider Figure 1, pencil in your name and list the ways you measure your self-esteem. What worldly values or pressures help determine your value? Who are the people you allow to help measure or determine your worth?

How I measure my self-esteem:

How God views me:

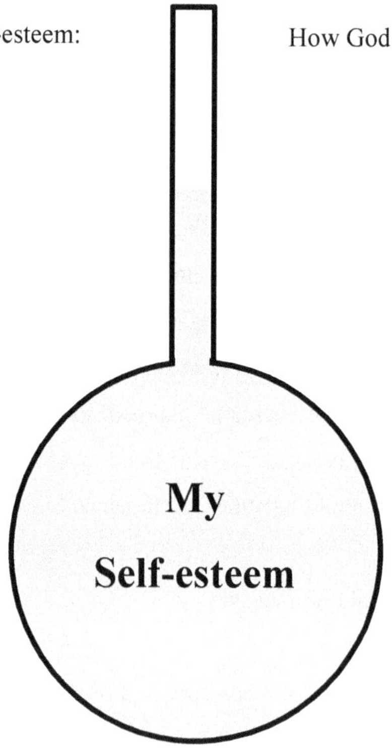

Figure 1

Review some of the truths you embraced in chapter 3 for your *ideal imago*. Use the right side of the thermometer to list these truths. These are the real measures of your value: you are loved, you are not a mistake, you have great potential, you are forgiven, you are not alone….
Are there others you need to put down here?

2. Now, use the space below to summarize what you have learned and what you want to hold onto. Do this by writing out your thoughts in the form of prayer to God. Here are some areas to consider:

   Roadblocks that try to stop me:
   Father, I see how much I compare myself with others and end up feeling insecure. I also measure my value by...

   People I am overly dependent on:
   I worry too much about what _______ thinks and not enough about what You think...

   Truths I want to embrace:
   I know You accept me the way I am; I don't have to perform for You...

   Anything else you want to tell God:
   Lord, I'd like to tell you about...

   Father, please forgive me for...

FOCUS — Read. Reflect. Pray. Do.

Psalm 23:1-3

The LORD is my shepherd, I shall not be in want. He makes me lie down in green pastures, He leads me beside quiet waters, He restores my soul. He guides me in paths of righteousness for His name's sake.

What is the main point of the passage?

How does it apply to me?

My Challenge Today

What challenges / opportunities await me today?

How do I want to respond to them?

My Focus Today

What is my guiding thought for today?

My Prayer Today

Specific things I am trusting God for:

For Further Study this Week

John 6:25-40, John 6:41-70, John 7:1-24, John 7:25-53, John 8:1-11, John 8:12-30

5 My Cup Runs Over

By now you've probably gotten the idea that the *Keep the Change!* process involves work, or effort. Of course, I hope you believe all of this work will be worthwhile, but we do need to admit that it does take effort to change old habits and to overcome past wounds.

> *Cast all your cares on Him, for He cares for you. – Peter, 1 Peter 5:7*

Just like running the roadblocks, it will require some work to look at our emotions and how they affect us. The best way I know how to help you do this is to introduce you to "the Cup." I think it will help you become more aware of what is going on in your emotional world.

Your Emotional Cup[1]

If you came to my office in Phoenix, I might offer you a glass of water. Imagine that after your drinking about one-half of your 12-ounce glass, I vanish to the kitchen and come back with a five-gallon bucket of water to refill your glass. We know only six-ounces will fit in the glass because it has a limited capacity, but I go ahead and pour freely from the bucket.

What happens? The glass fills up, then it overflows, then we have a puddle on the floor, then you may think about leaving! Seriously, if I pour in the whole five gallons, we will have quite a mess.

In the same way, each of us carries an invisible cup with us all of the time. You've had this cup your whole life. It isn't a cup of water, it is a cup

---

[1] Based, in part, on David Ferguson's Intimate Encounters, pg. 18. I have expanded on this concept.

of your emotions. Just like the cup of water, if you overfill your cup, you end up with a mess.

Everyone has good and bad things happen in life, leading to positive and negative emotions. Positive emotions include things like enjoying loving relationships, faith, fun events, laughter and thankfulness. Negative emotions may include feelings of frustration, anger, boredom and fear.

Each day's events add to your cup, leaving you with a sense of fulfillment if most feelings have been positive; or feeling down and gloomy if several negative emotions have gathered in your cup. If you did nothing about these feelings, you would be exhausted and overwhelmed very quickly.

Can you visualize the water level of the cup rising? You ultimately will spill over if you don't find a way to lower your water level. These "spills" we have are typically negative emotions like anger, anxiety and discouragement.

Spills are usually symptoms rather than the root causes. They can be normal reactions like frustration and anger. They can also become quite serious like depression, anxiety attacks, violent or abusive anger, or addictive behaviors. If you are facing some spills where you are acting inappropriately, you know how important it is to get these symptoms under control. You may even benefit from attending a support group or seeing a counselor or therapist. Ultimately, though, you'll need to address the root causes.

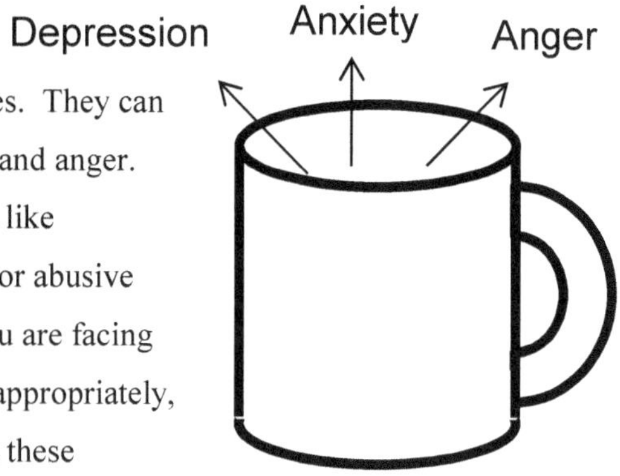

Now, envision you have a relief spout on the side of your cup, preventing your water level from getting too high. It's an "overflow preventer" which releases water as you process emotions. Imagine how the level falls again as you process the emotions. We usually deal with the things in our cup without even thinking about it.

Each of us needs healthy ways to deal with the events and experiences of the day. We see this in school children. Kids use playtime to process what they are learning and experiencing about their world. That's one reason recess is important for their emotional health.

Adults need healthy ways to process their feelings, too. We use a variety of activities to deal with the feelings in "the cup." For example, exercise can be very beneficial to your mental health. As you move your body and burn off calories, you are literally blowing off some steam. When you talk to a friend about a situation or when you go for a walk, you are processing emotion. When you discuss your day with your partner, you are dealing with the day's events and emotions.

There are an almost unlimited number of ways to process life and emotions. We listen to music, read the Bible, pray, pursue hobbies or serve other people. What do you do?

Exercise 5

When you are under stress, what helps you relax?

When you face a setback or discouragement, what helps you process things?

I Got A Rock

Remember when Charlie Brown went trick-or-treating? Each of the kids held out their bags expectantly. The other children got candy, apples and other sweet stuff. Charlie Brown "got a rock."

As we go through life, we get rocks, just like Charlie Brown. The rocks in our emotional cups are scars, hurts and setbacks which don't seem to go away. They are your unresolved issues. You probably don't think about them all of the time. In fact, you may not think about them much at all. But, they take up room in your cup.

Imagine if your cup had eight or ten large rocks in it. There wouldn't be much room for the water! That's right, when you are carrying around several unresolved issues, you don't have as much room for your normal emotions. Your typical up's and down's will then cause you to spill over very easily.

John was a man in his 30's dealing with volcano-like anger. He could hold it inside for weeks, then would erupt in anger at his wife and kids, often for no apparent reason. Before his anger problem, he had struggled with drugs, alcohol abuse and low self-esteem.

All of these symptoms, or spills, were connected to a cup full of rocks John had been carrying around for over 20 years. When he was 15, his relationship with his father became so bad that he moved out and lived on his own (Rock #1). Then, at 17, his girlfriend was tragically killed and he had no one to help him through the grief (Rock #2). In his 20's, John dabbled in drugs and drifted from job to job. After losing his relationship with his dad, losing his girlfriend and losing several jobs, John felt like a big-time loser (Rock #3)!

> *Do not get drunk on wine, which leads to debauchery. Instead, be filled with the Spirit. – Paul, Ephesians 6:18*

Not knowing what to do with the rocks, John turned even more to alcohol and drugs (spills). He tried to make it stop hurting, if only for a few hours. Imagine the frustration and resentment and emotional pain he carried inside.

Rocks and Spills

Do you see the inter-connection between the rocks and the spills? The rocks max out your emotional capacity, leaving you with emotional pain. When normal life events add to your cup, you easily spill over. The three most common reactions (spills) to a cup full of pain are to explode in anger, distract yourself in some way or suppress your emotions and hold them inside.

People often get angry when they are hurting. Some erupt in violent or loud anger. Others control their anger or express it more quietly. Either way, these anger spills can destroy our relationships and our lives, if left unchecked. Ten minutes of anger can brutally damage the best of relationships. If you find yourself getting angry too often or too intensely, it's time to ask what is going on inside your cup.

All people distract themselves at times and takes their mind off their concerns. That is normal. There are many healthy distractions: reading a book, exercise, enjoying a meal.... However, we are easily tempted to go overboard with the distractions as a way of coping with emotional pain.

For example, you might enjoy a glass of wine at the end of the day. It helps you relax and unwind. But, if you start to use alcohol as a way to forget the pain, you head down a dangerous path. Once you begin using alcohol, food, drugs, sex or shopping as a means to cope with life, you have to keep repeating the behavior of distracting yourself. From there, it is easy to become addicted to the substance or behavior.

When you get hooked on something, in essence you are making that thing your god. It becomes too important in your life. You give control of your life to that drug or activity. Rather than serving God, you become enmeshed in continuing the counter-productive behavior. So, the distraction that felt so good and helped you forget your problems only ends up complicating your life and multiplying your problems and pain.

The third common response to a full emotional cup is to suppress your emotions. When you stuff them inside and ignore your pain, it's like holding 50 ping pong balls under water. You may be able to do it for a while, but you will ultimately fail.

When people suppress their negative emotions, they inadvertently suppress their ability to experience their positive emotions as well. They often feel numb and out of touch with their feelings. Eventually, the pressure inside becomes too intense and they either erupt in anger or have an emotional meltdown.

By suppressing your feelings long-term, you set yourself up for problems with depression and anxiety. Just like addictions or anger issues, these symptoms can easily take on a life of their own. If you have ever been through a period of depression, you know how debilitating it can be.

So, the rocks are taking up space, the emotions are overwhelming us and the spills are making a mess of our lives. None of that is very encouraging! But, don't give up yet. Things are about to get better. It's time to start dealing with the Cup.

How to Deal with the Rocks

At the end of this chapter, your homework is to begin dealing with your rocks. Here are four words that can help you:

Show: Deal with your rocks by first identifying them. Label the rocks. What hurts? What issues aren't resolved? What relationships aren't right?

When you put it on paper, you begin the healing process by no longer suppressing or ignoring the issues.

Throw: 1 Peter 5:7 tells us to cast our cares on Him, because He cares for us. Envision throwing your rocks away from yourself. Throw them off your shoulders and onto God. Write about them (journaling), pray about them and let go of the pain. You can also throw them off by sharing them with others who will listen to you and support you.

Know: Know you aren't alone. God has promised to "never leave you or forsake you" (Joshua 1:8, Hebr 13:5). When you remember His presence and the support of friends, it will help you to not give up and better handle the rocks.

Go: Take action. Deal with the rocks by journaling, talking with friends, writing a letter to those involved, confronting or forgiving those involved. Ultimately, go on with life when you feel you've addressed the rocks as best as you can.

Life-Changer #5

SHOW - Draw and Label your Cup

Take some time and reflect on your emotional life. What rocks are in your cup? What issues do you have that don't go away? Pain from the past? Disappointments? Hurting relationships? Draw the rocks and identify them. Give them names.

Figure 2: My Cup

THROW - Get it off your Chest

Journal by writing about one rock / day. Write out your prayers, tell God how this rock has affected you, how it hurts and what you wish was different.... Talk to a friend this week about one of the rocks. Ask him/her to listen without giving you advice.

KNOW – What you Need to Remember

Choose a favorite Bible verse that helps you keep perspective, or choose from this list:

1 Peter 5:7, Joshua 1:8; Hebrews 13:5, Deuteronomy 31:6-8, John 3:16.

Write that favorite verse out here:

What I have learned:

What I need to remember:

GO – Act on it, Move ahead

What do you need to do now? Write someone a letter? Confront a situation? Journal some more? Seek out help?

What I need to do now:

Focus — Read. Reflect. Pray. Do.

Psalm 23:4-6

Even though I walk through the valley of the shadow of death,[l] *I will fear no evil, for You are with me; Your rod and Your staff, they comfort me.*

You prepare a table before me in the presence of my enemies. You anoint my head with oil; my cup overflows.

Surely goodness and love will follow me all the days of my life, and I will dwell in the house of the Lord forever.

What is the main point of the passage?

How does it apply to me?

My Challenge Today

What challenges / opportunities await me today?

How do I want to respond to them?

My Focus Today

What is my guiding thought for today?

My Prayer Today

Specific things I am trusting God for:

For Further Study this Week

1 Peter 5:1-11, Eph.6:10-20, John 8:31-58, John 9:1-12, John 9:13-41, Romans 12:1-8

6 Making Peace with Your Past

In 1991, the movie *City Slickers* touched a nerve with middle-aging Baby Boomers. Billy Crystal told us, "Your life is a do-over; you've got a clean slate." As the movie progressed, Crystal and his buddies determined to "do-over," to reassess their lives and their regrets, then decide which parts to keep and which parts to do differently.

> *If possible, as far as it depends on you, live at peace with all.*
> *– Paul, Romans 12:18*

Do you want a do-over? As I reflect back over decisions I've made, people I've disappointed, mistakes I've committed, bad things that have happened…it leads me to one question: What am I waiting for? I want that do-over right now!

Maybe you are thinking, we all want to start over, but it doesn't work that way. You are right, there are many things that hold us back from the fresh start we are considering. One of the big obstacles, or roadblocks, keeping us from moving forward is our past. Look at these three ways the past holds us back.

Old Wounds

Many of us have been wounded badly in the past. These old wounds probably have healed to some degree, but they leave scars. They are like a splinter you get in your hand that gets infected. Sometimes it festers and oozes, because there is still something down in the wound that hasn't come out yet. Disgusting!

Do you know someone who is hurting about something that happened long ago? Maybe you yourself are? Just ignoring it and hoping it will go away doesn't work. At some point, you have to open up the wound and get the bad stuff out. That's what we'll work on in a few minutes. Don't worry, it won't be as painful as getting the sliver out of your hand when you were a kid.

Poor Choices

We all made big mistakes growing up. Every teen-ager makes bad choices. Most of us have something we really regret, something we wished we hadn't done. Often, that decision led to someone else getting hurt or offended.

Exercise 6

What comes to mind when you think about the poor decisions you have made? Which one do you have the most regrets about? Who else got hurt?

The flip-side of making wrong choices and hurting others is what we tend to do afterwards: We feel guilty and beat ourselves up. What guilt do you still carry around? How do you beat yourself up about it?

Resentment, Anger and Other Fun Stuff

Everyone has bad stuff happen to them. There are things which haven't gone your way. Things that shouldn't have happened have happened to you. People have let you down, disappointed you and lied to you.

The bottom-line: these setbacks are not just frustrating, they make us angry. It's not fair! You ask, "Why me? What did I do to deserve this?" If left unchecked, your anger can morph into long-term resentment and bitterness.

Sound familiar? These old wounds, wrong choices and bad experiences leave us with a past we'd like to forget, but don't. The temptation is to ignore the past and hope time will heal the wounds. Sometimes it does; often it doesn't, especially the big hurts. That's why you need to process and make peace with your past.

Process Your Past

Growing up, my mother had a small oak cabinet on the wall of her kitchen. This cabinet had several tiny drawers with little knobs. There were no labels on the outside of the drawers, so I had no idea what was in them. I would crawl up on the kitchen counter-top, so I could reach the mysterious cabinet and open the drawers one-by-one and sniff what was in there. Inside one was cinnamon stick, others had clove, nutmeg...it was a spice cabinet.

We often store old wounds like my mom stored spices. We put away the pain in little drawers of our memory where it resides until something bumps it open. The pain doesn't get processed, it just hangs around.

Rather than ignoring what hurts and storing up the wounds in a cabinet, it is much better if we identify and expose the old hurts. We can then process them and put them away in a healthier fashion. That's what I want to help you do now.

Identify the Pain of the Past

As we saw before in 1 Peter 5:7, God want us to turn over our concerns, pain and worries to Him:

Cast all your cares upon Him, for He cares about you.

God has promised to lift your burdens if you give them to Him. You can't give Him your burdens, though, if you aren't in touch with what they are. In order to get His help, the first thing you need to do is to identify what hurts, what you regret, what you beat yourself up about, who hurt you....

Exercise 7

Go ahead and list those regrets, wounds and pain here:

Leave to Grieve

Those wounds and choices have kept you from moving ahead with your life. They have held you back and kept you from what could have been. But, we are often so busy with life that we can't or don't make time to stop and process the past. I want to give you permission, and encouragement, to take a time-out and allow yourself to "leave to grieve." If you take an hour or two now to grieve over the past, it will pay off for you in the future.

Let's review the basics of the grief cycle. Then, I'll have you identify where you are in the grief process regarding your past.

The Grief Cycle

Grieving is a process we all need to go through at different points in life. When we lose a loved one, we need to grieve the loss. It is the process of emotionally coming to grips with what has happened and adjusting to the future reality.

When you lose something or someone important, like a family member or a career or a relationship, you are confronted by a reality you don't like. You didn't choose for this to happen. It was done to you by someone or something else. Something very valuable has been taken from you and you'll never get it back.

There are four phases of grief. Here is a quick explanation about each of them:

The first phase of grief is **shock**. You may be stunned about what has happened, like someone hit you between the eyes. People in shock are easily overwhelmed and may be out of touch with reality. It is important to keep other people around you when you are in this phase. You need their support and guidance.

After this initial phase, you may find yourself in **denial**. You don't believe the loss will be so bad after all. Or, you think maybe everything will really turn out okay Or, you find yourself repeating the story over and over again, as you try to come to grips with what actually happened. While in denial, it is very helpful to find someone who will listen to you talk about your loss. Explain to them you don't need a lot of answers, you just need them to listen to and support you.

As you move further along in grief, you end up at the bottom in the phase I call **confused emotions**. This is when you flip-flop between a variety of emotions. You are "all over the board." You may be happy, sad, lonely, angry and then happy again, all in just a few hours' time!

In this time of confusion, the best thing you can do is journal about what you are feeling. Write out your prayers and tell God what is on your heart. Give the burden to Him and ask His help every day. Also, keep reminding yourself that this is a phase you are going through, you won't be on such an emotional roller coaster forever!

Finally, you move on to the phase of **adjusting** to the new reality. You come to **accept** what has happened and you adapt over time to life that is different than it was in the past.

The frustrating thing about grief is that it isn't predictable and it isn't a one-way street. You don't know if your denial will take a week or a month to work through. You may think you are coping and adjusting pretty well, and then find yourself back in denial or in confused emotions again.

I believe a key to grief is just accepting that the process will be confusing. It will take time and it is unpredictable. Another key is to remember you aren't alone. God has promised to never leave you. Even if you don't feel His presence, He is there and wants to help you. Hang onto this truth, even in the tough times.

Where are You?

Now that you have identified your hurts and regrets, where are you in the grief process concerning these things? Even if something happened a long time ago, have you grieved over it? Have you worked through the pain and come to accept it? Use Fig. 3 and indicate with an "x" what point you are at with the different things you need to grieve.

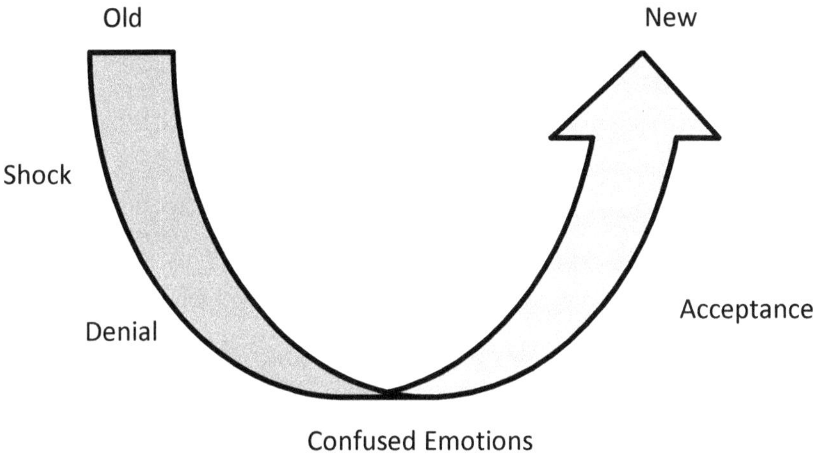

Figure 3: The Grief Cycle

What to Do Now

Soon after the 9/11 terrorist attacks, I was contacted by a company which had lost many of its employees on an upper floor of the World Trade Center. The company asked me to hold a seminar about grief for their employees at their branch in Phoenix.

Each of the "survivors" was experiencing grief differently. Some were in shock. Others were feeling guilty for surviving. Others were doing their best to distance themselves from the situation.

Although your loss is different than those employees, the principles are the same. Here are the key points I shared with them:

Steps to Working through Loss:

1. Recognize this is normal. This is a process. It takes time to work through.
2. Acknowledge your loss. What I lost… How I felt last week… How I feel now…
3. Admit your anger/pain:
4. Tell your story to others.
5. Exercise!!!
6. Comfort someone else. Listen to their story. Remember: don't give pat answers. Every one grieves differently; let them share; learn from them.
7. Remember, grief is a process. It can affect you for some time.
8. Celebrate your growth. Create something beautiful. Do something positive. Be creative. Volunteer. Become/create a living memorial.
9. Tell your story again.

Life-Changer #6: Where to Go from Here

1. Before you move on to the next chapter, I recommend you do three things. First, go back and re-read this chapter. Highlight the things that were most important to you.

2. Next, use the space below to write out a personal summary in the form of a prayer. Tell God about the wounds and regrets you have. Identify where you are in grieving them. From the list above, decide what the next step for you should be. Ask His help in processing the past.

3. Share these thoughts with someone you trust. Tell him/her how you feel, what hurts and how you hope to move ahead. It will help you immensely and it may also be of great help to the other person as well.

4. Continue your daily FOCUS time.

FOCUS — Read. Reflect. Pray. Do.

Psalm 25:1-5

In You, LORD my God, I put my trust.
I trust in You; do not let me be put to shame, nor let my enemies triumph over me. No one who hopes in You will ever be put to shame, but shame will come on those who are treacherous without cause. Show me Your ways, Lord, teach me Your paths.
Guide me in Your truth and teach me, for You are God my Savior, and my hope is in You all day long.

What is the main point of the passage?

How does it apply to me?

My Challenge Today

What challenges / opportunities await me today?

How do I want to respond to them?

My Focus Today

What is my guiding thought for today?

My Prayer Today

Specific things I am trusting God for:

For Further Study this Week

Romans 12:9-21, John 10:1-21, John 10:22-42, John 11:1-16, John 11:17-44, John 11:45-57

7 Freedom through Forgiveness

Now that we have identified the rocks, hurts and pain from the past, we come to the next step of processing and healing the past by beginning to forgive.

> *Therefore, as God's chosen people, holy and dearly loved, clothe yourselves with compassion, kindness, humility, gentleness and patience. Bear with each other and forgive one another. Forgive as the Lord forgave you.*
> *- Paul, Colossians 3:12-13*

I once met a successful banker in his 50's who invited me in to his apartment. Looking around, it was obvious the home had a woman's touch, so I asked "Where is your wife?" He responded, "Oh, ah…she left me recently for another man…for a 20-year old man!"

After hearing how his wife of many years had left, I thought it might not be long until she tired of the young man, so I asked him, "If she comes back to you, will you be able to forgive her?"

He looked at me, shrugged his shoulders and asked, "What's to forgive? We'll just try to move ahead and forget about it."

What do you think about that? Can a couple just pretend something like that never happened and go on with life successfully? I've shared this story with lots of people. Almost everyone agrees it wouldn't go well with the married couple unless they talk things over and find a way to resolve and forgive.

The story of that couple reminds me of an important principle:

Unless we find forgiveness, we'll never truly be free to become what we can become.

When someone has hurt you or deeply disappointed you, unless you find a way to clear the air, there will always be something in the way of a healthy relationship. You'll grow distant from one another. Instead of harmony and peace, resentment, anger and bitterness enter your life when you don't forgive.

Think about how you feel when you harm someone or let them down. Do you remember what that guilt feels like? Guilt hurts, it makes us feel bad about ourselves. We don't like to be reminded of our shortcomings, so we are tempted to avoid it and deny any wrongdoing at all. If we avoid seeking forgiveness, we create distance and pain.

Without forgiveness, we are prisoners of the wounds we endure or the guilt we carry. We need to forgive and we need to be forgiven…but how do we do that?

Forgiveness: What it is and what it isn't

When our children were young, they had an old tractor tire as a sandbox in our backyard. I remember watching the kids play, thinking how cute it was to see our two-year-old Andy lean over the tire to barely touch the sand with his shovel. He was playing so well with his big sister…until I turned away for a moment. I'll let you listen in from here…

"Daddy, Andy just threw sand in my eyes!"

"eeee-no-eeee"

"Andy, did you throw sand?"

"eeee-no-eeee"

"Yes, he did, Daddy…and it hurts real bad."

"I think you did…Andy, say you're sorry."

Andy then turns stiff as a board, stamps his feet and shouts

"SOR-REEE!!"

That's probably not the best example of great parenting! It's also not the best example of forgiveness. Andy may have said some words, but not much repenting and not much forgiveness happened there.

The word "forgive" means to release, to let something go. Like opening your fist and allowing a big rock to drop to the ground, you forgive when you don't hang onto a wound. You choose to let it go. You release it. You forgive.

Why is Forgiveness such a Big Deal?

The most beautiful story of forgiveness I know is found in Luke's gospel, where a young man demands and then squanders his inheritance. After bottoming out in life, he comes to his senses:

> *I will set out and go back to my father and say to him: Father, I have sinned against heaven and against you. I am no longer worthy to be called your son; make me like one of your hired men.*
> *–Luke 15:18-19*

The remarkable thing about this story is the father's response:

> *But while he was still a long way off, his father saw him and was filled with compassion for him; he ran to his son, threw his arms around him and kissed him. – v. 20*

Rather than focus on his son's mistakes and make him jump through hoops to somehow earn back favor, the father runs to the son and accepts him…just as he is! Once the son came back, the father forgave and restored the relationship.

Jesus told us this story so we can understand how great God's love is for us. Each of us strays and makes wrong choices. We let ourselves and others down. We let God down. Yet, in spite of our sin, God wants to restore the relationship.

That's why forgiveness is a big deal. In order to restore the relationship, we need forgiveness. That's why He sent His Son for us. Jesus didn't come merely to be a good example or to teach us a better way of living; rather He came to sacrifice His life, to pay the penalty for our sins and to restore our relationship with God.

By receiving God's forgiveness, you are set free: Free from the debt and guilt that stand between you and the Father; free to become the best You you can become; free to forgive others; free to walk in harmony with God and with those He brings into your life.

The Flip Side

Before we get to the Life-Changer worksheet for this chapter, let's look at one other aspect of forgiveness.

Lasting forgiveness requires a commitment to changed behavior.

Imagine if you met a friend for coffee. Then, after the visit your friend walks you out to your car. While waving good-bye, you back your car up and drive over his foot! Of course you stop and quickly apologize. You say how truly sorry you are and that you didn't intend to hurt him. He waives it off and hobbles away. The following week you meet for coffee again. You ask about his foot and he assures you he is recovering. At the end of the visit, he walks you out to the car again. You then back up and drive over his foot again! You stop and quickly apologize again, stating you didn't intend to hurt him.

Will your friend be willing to forgive again? Maybe, but it will be a lot harder. Even if you didn't intend it, he still got hurt. You said the words, but you didn't act to protect his foot. He will no longer trust you or your driving!

The flip side of repentance and seeking forgiveness is *changed behavior*. Without change, trust will be destroyed, limiting your future relationship with your friend. Instead, if you take care to not hurt your friend and show him you care about him and his foot, trust can begin to grow again.

In the same way, genuine repentance before God or others calls for you to make a genuine effort to change. You take steps so it won't happen again. Otherwise, you are just wasting your time.

How to Make Forgiveness Work for You

We've considered several aspects of forgiveness. The bottom-line is we need to forgive and we need to be forgiven, but we often don't want to do either. Now, let's make this very practical.

> *When you think of forgiveness, think of three words:*
> *Confess, Express, Request.*

Confess: Admit to something and to call it by name.

We like to be very vague and general about our mistakes; we try to minimize the extent of the wrongs we commit. We also tend to "weasel out" and not admit the wrong we've done, but this only causes more pain.

Don't do this! Man up! Be man enough or woman enough to specifically say what you did and how it was wrong. That's right, you need to go to the offended person and say it out loud. Then, STOP! Don't give excuses. Don't justify your actions. Don't hint at how someone else is to blame. Just admit the wrong and then stop talking for a moment.

Express: Express *sorrow* and a *commitment to change.*

When you express sorrow over what happened, you acknowledge the hurt you have caused. There isn't anything you can do to undo your wrong, but you can validate the other person's feelings by recognizing the pain you caused.

Also, express your genuine commitment to change your behavior. Briefly explain what steps you will take to see that it won't happen again. Your friend doesn't need an ironclad guarantee as much as to hear from you that you are serious about changing.

Request: A brief statement asking for forgiveness.

Saying "I'm sorry" isn't a request. It is often a declaration people yelp when they get caught. You may be saying sorry because you got caught or because someone is upset with you. Like Andy when he threw sand at his sister, saying "I'm sorry" often isn't a genuine request for forgiveness.

Instead, try these five words: *Would you please forgive me?*
You can't make someone forgive you, you can only do all that is in your power to seek forgiveness and the restoration of the relationship.

The Key to Forgiveness

Forgiveness is tough stuff. It is hard to admit your wrongs and go to someone and seek forgiveness. It can also be extremely hard to accept someone's apology and extend forgiveness. That's because the whole issue of forgiveness is deeply spiritual. Without God's help, you won't be good at forgiving or seeking forgiveness. Look at this next passage:

> *Bear with each other and forgive one another... Forgive as the Lord forgave you.* - Paul, Colossians 3:13

Do you see the command here, to forgive in the same manner He forgave you? How did God forgive you? Was it because you deserved forgiveness or because you are a great person? No, God offers forgiveness as an undeserved gift to those who believe in and rely on Jesus for forgiveness.

We don't deserve forgiveness, yet God offers it to us as a gift. In the same way, we are called to extend the gift of forgiveness to those who offend us. We forgive, not because we feel forgiving, but because we choose to forgive and release the anger and resentment. You can forgive, even if the other person never comes back to apologize to you. Just make the choice to forgive, it will lighten your load.

When you choose to forgive like God forgives you or when you choose to seek forgiveness, something very special happens. You are becoming more godly. You become free. You are choosing to follow in the steps of Jesus and forgive as He does. Just imagine how you will be blessed and changed as you follow Him in this way!

Life-Changer #7

I've given you three worksheets to help you with forgiveness. Start by seeking God's forgiveness. Use the first one to guide your thoughts as you seek a better relationship with Him. Use the next page to prepare to seek someone else's forgiveness. Use the last page to prepare to forgive someone else.

Personally Experience Forgiveness

"Forgive as the Lord forgave you" -Colossians 3:13

Have I personally experienced God's forgiveness?

a. Confess the Wrong.

What I need to confess to God:

b. Express Sorrow.
Talk to God about my regret:

c. Express a Commitment to Change.
What I plan to do differently:

How I need His help:

d. Request Forgiveness: ask God to forgive you.
Dear Father, would you please forgive me for…

Seek Forgiveness from Someone Else

a. **Confess the Wrong.**
What I need to confess to ____________?

b. **Express Sorrow.**
How my actions harmed him/her:

c. **Express a Commitment to Change.**
How I plan to change this:

d. **Request Forgiveness:**
Would you please forgive me for…

How To Forgive Someone

- **Get alone for a while to reflect on the situation.**
  - write down specifically what that person did.
  - write down what was wrong about it.

- **Talk it over:**
  - first with God.
  - then with the other person –if possible.
  (Share your feelings without accusing).

- **Offer forgiveness**
  - as a gift (forgiveness isn't earned).
  - put it behind you.
  - never bring it up again.
  - burn the paper.

Whom do I need to forgive?

What did he/she do? What was wrong about it?

When will we talk about it?

When will I "release it and let it go"?

"Forgive as the Lord forgave you" -Colossians 3:13

Focus — Read. Reflect. Pray. Do.

Psalm 37:1-4

Do not fret because of those who are evil or be envious of those who do wrong; for like the grass they will soon wither, like green plants they will soon die away. Trust in the LORD and do good; dwell in the land and enjoy safe pasture. Take delight in the LORD, and He will give you the desires of your heart.

What is the main point of the passage?

How does it apply to me?

My Challenge Today

What challenges / opportunities await me today?

How do I want to respond to them?

My Focus Today

What is my guiding thought for today?

My Prayer Today

Specific things I am trusting God for:

For Further Study this Week

Colossians 3:12-13, Luke 15:11-20, Luke 15:21-31, John 12:1-11, John 12:12-36, John 12:37-50

Part 3

Building a Strong Foundation for Change

8 Building Your Life on the Right Values

Growing up in central Illinois 100 years after his death, I frequently felt in the shadow of Abraham Lincoln. We visited his boyhood home in New Salem, played "free the slaves" in our backyards and wore coonskin caps.[2] Eventually, I moved on to more exciting heroes like Superman.

> *Be sure you put your feet in the right place, then stand firm.*
> *– Abraham Lincoln*

However, as an adult, I came back to Lincoln, reading several histories of his life. While not perfect by any measure, Lincoln made momentous decisions while under enormous pressures.

In 1862, in the midst of the Civil War, Lincoln faced a watershed-type decision. It was especially difficult because he had to choose between two values which appeared diametrically opposed to one another.

Prior to the Secession, Lincoln had made it his priority to keep the Union together, even if it meant tolerating slavery in the southern states. He held firmly to the value that the American states needed one another and belonged together. In 1858, while running for Senator, he gave his famous "House Divided" speech. "A house divided against itself cannot stand."

The second value was the abolition of slavery. As early as 1849, Lincoln believed slavery should be abolished. By the time he was elected President in 1860, the abolitionists had become increasingly vocal, demanding abolition, regardless of whether the South would accept it.

---

[2] I don't think Abe ever wore a coonskin cap. I think we got the legends of Daniel Boone and Lincoln confused, but we Illinois boys didn't really care.

Lincoln was caught between these two opposing values, both of which seemed vitally important. He ultimately chose to abolish slavery through the Emancipation Proclamation.

Beliefs and Values

While most of us don't face major political decisions affecting millions of people, each of us is confronted by choices and decisions to make daily. The decisions we make are based on the beliefs and values we hold, whether we are aware of them or not.

When you put on a scarf in the winter, it may be partly based on your beliefs and values. You may believe a scarf around your neck will prevent you from getting sick; not getting sick may be something you highly value. Or, you may believe the scarf is fashionable and you value looking good out in public.

There is often a fine line in the difference between beliefs and values. They tend to overlap, so let's not spend too much time splitting hairs. For our discussion, let's look at it this way:

> *Your beliefs guide your values which influence your emotions which affect your behaviors.*

Looking at it succinctly: Beliefs ➔values ➔emotions ➔behaviors. Many of our beliefs and values are subtle. We don't know where we got them. They are partly cultural, partly from family, partly personal and partly worldly. We've looked at beliefs in an earlier chapter, so let's focus on values now.

Competing Values

What is important to you? What do you most value in life? Would you agree that your everyday behaviors often don't match up with the things you say you value? Most of us are like that. We allow outside influences to draw us away from our core values and commitments, or we get distracted and forget what is most important.

Sarah claimed to be highly committed to living responsibly with her family. Part of that included being financially responsibly. She and her husband were committed to living within their means. Yet, Sarah's actions didn't back this up. She regularly overspent her monthly budget by hundreds of dollars on designer clothes.

Obviously, Sarah had competing values. There was something else that seemed more important than staying within her budget. She held another value: Sarah felt her worth as a person depended on "looking good." She was convinced she needed new fancy clothes to look good and feel good about herself.

I'm assuming you have good intentions for yourself and for those God brings into your life. You aren't plotting to hurt others and your ultimate goal in life isn't to sit on a pile of gold while watching others starve! You probably don't even have your primary focus on shallow things like owning the fanciest car in the lot or being the most beautiful or powerful in town. Am I right?

However, even if you have great motives and good values, you are susceptible to having those values compromised. There are dozens of forces that try to distract you or influence you each day. Let's brainstorm a bit on influences that compete with your values. I've started a partial list, please take a few moments and add to them.

Exercise 7: What Competes with My Values

Marketing / retailers:

-"buy it now, don't pay for 180 days"

-"you deserve a break today"

-"come to the happiest place on earth"

-"what happens in Vegas, stays in Vegas"

-take a drug for what ails you[3]

-

-

-

Media / film[4]:

-beauty isn't just skin deep, it's everything.

-marriage is optional / disposable.

-"don't worry, be happy"

-escape from reality is good, even necessary.

-

-

---

[3] Watch the TV commercials for the evening news; over 75% of these commercials call people to buy medications. As America ages, more services appear to minimize pain, stop aging.... The message is that drugs will solve your problems.

[4] The top 10 highest-grossing films in 2010 all offered a different form of reality, either animated or mystical. What is the value these films embrace? To escape, leave reality behind?

Society / World:

-commitment is an option.

-marriages and families are disposable.

-your value is based on: a) money; b) beauty; c) power; d) a, b and c.

-bigger is better

-only focus on your own needs

-everyone should own a home

-freedom means doing whatever I want

-accumulate wealth / accumulate things

-

-

-

Family Values: what values do you embrace from your family?

-

-

-

-

➔ Circle the values above that influence you the most.

➔ Put an * by the values you want to influence you the most.

The Challenge: Choosing and Living out Values

Remember what we discussed before?

Your beliefs guide your values which influence your emotions which affect your behaviors.

The values you choose will determine how you feel about life. They will also drive your behaviors. On the previous page, you identified many values from the outside world which try to influence your personal values and behaviors.

For these reasons, it is vital to be deliberate and to wisely choose what is most important to you. But, this type of deliberate thinking is counter-cultural, running contrary to much of what we hear. We are told to go with the flow, to be tolerant without thinking critically. It can be hard work to discern and stand up for what is right. It is often unpopular to cling to values not embraced by the mainstream.

However, if you don't challenge society's values, you will easily be swept along, sucked into the commonly-accepted, politically-correct view of life. From there, it is easy to drift into mediocrity, adopting a lifestyle and values that, while widely-accepted, won't lead you to the meaningful life of blessing that you intend.

Of course, we don't intrinsically have the correct values we need to base life on. This is where we need God's input and direction. I have found the Bible to be more than a fascinating read and source of comfort. It is literally God's spoken word, providing us with direction and values, as well as a living relationship with God.

While biblical literacy is no guarantee for successful living, I frequently observe how many mistakes we make, simply because we don't know or don't apply God's directions for our lives. Even among committed Christians, the numbers of those doing in-depth Bible study has declined drastically. Beyond superficial skimming or listening to sermons, many of us are too busy to seek out God's Word.

When you follow God's Word and take His advice, life turns out better.

This is so simple, but so true! When you use the Bible to shape your values, you buy into the idea that God is wiser than you and your life will turn out better when you listen to Him. Your values become more like God's values, leading you to a productive life of love and blessing to others. Who doesn't want that?

Jeremy and Allison discovered how easy it is to get swept along. They began their young marriage like most of their friends, a combination of work, faith, television, materialism and social events. Over time, they acquired more things, became extremely busy and began drifting from God and from one another. Their strong values on their faith and their marriage were challenged.

But, Jeremy and Allison woke up. They didn't give in to the pressures of society and life. They chose to not become another divorce statistic in-the-making. Instead, they did something bold and courageous: they gave away their television! They exchanged the time with the t.v. for time with one another. They also got active with their faith, joining a Bible study group and serving in their church. As they changed their priorities to reflect their values, they grew closer to one another and felt more satisfied in life.

As you reflect on the values you have embraced and determine which are most important to you, you may face difficult choices like President Lincoln. By choosing the values that will define your life, your priorities will become clearer, leading you to better choices.

Before you use Life-Changer #8 to guide you in your selection of core values, please review chapters 1-8. Pay special attention to the answers you've given to the previous Life-Changer worksheets. What patterns do you see? What are you learning?

Life-Changer #8 What Do You Value?

Outside values:

Refer back to the worksheet you completed on pg. 74-75. List below the outside values that have most influenced you. Cross out the ones you want to reject.

What God values:

Use the Bible verses quoted in chapters1-8 and others you know. List the key verses and what He says here:

What I value: (re: family, work, faith, character, service…)

Write out your values, what is most important to you:

➔ Review this last list. Put a * by the ones that are the biggest challenge to you, where you need to place special attention.

➔ Write your values out on a 3 x 5 card. Carry it with you this week. Pray daily for God to help you embrace and live out these values.

Focus — Read. Reflect. Pray. Do.

Psalm 37: 5-7

Commit your way to the LORD; trust in Him and He will do this: He will make your righteous reward shine like the dawn, your vindication like the noonday sun. Be still before the LORD and wait patiently for Him.

What is the main point of the passage?

How does it apply to me?

My Challenge Today

What challenges / opportunities await me today?

How do I want to respond to them?

My Focus Today

What is my guiding thought for today?

My Prayer Today

Specific things I am trusting God for:

For Further Study this Week

John 13:1-17, John 13:18-30, John 13:31-38, John 14:1-14, John 14:15-31, John 15:1-8

9 Life with Purpose

Ten years ago, I became interested in genealogy. I searched the internet and used genealogy websites to discover my roots. After I had exhausted researching the Zimmerman family tree, I began looking into Barbara's, my wife.

> *The purpose of life is a life of purpose. —Robert Byrne*

As I dug into the Briggs and Rigg family histories, I discovered something very fascinating: of the 102 passengers on the Mayflower, two of them were in Barbara's family tree, one on each side! That got me to thinking more about those pilgrims.

Did you know the Mayflower Pilgrims came from both Holland and England? Most were English Dissenters, puritan Christians who had rejected the Church of England. They had placed a high **value** on freedom of worship. This value was so important to them, it gave rise to a **vision**, the dream of living in freedom and establishing a colony where they could worship freely and have their church without outside control. Ultimately, they found a **vehicle** (the Mayflower) to take them on their **voyage,** travelling to the New World where they established their new colony.

Although most of us will never make such a perilous voyage, each of us needs to go through the process of choosing a life direction. Let's look at it more closely.

Values ➔ Vision (Purpose) ➔ Vehicle ➔ Voyage

Last chapter, you examined your values. Your values are based on your beliefs and influence your emotions and behaviors. I hope this was helpful and you will continue to fine-tune your understanding on what is most important to you in life, what values you will hold fast. Just like the Pilgrims, your values should also drive your vision, or purpose. Let's look at this more closely.

Purpose and Needs

Choosing your purpose is closely linked to your needs as a person. For some background, let's look at what others think. Psychologists have studied, argued and formed theories about the subject of human needs for centuries. One of the most influential was Abraham Maslow.

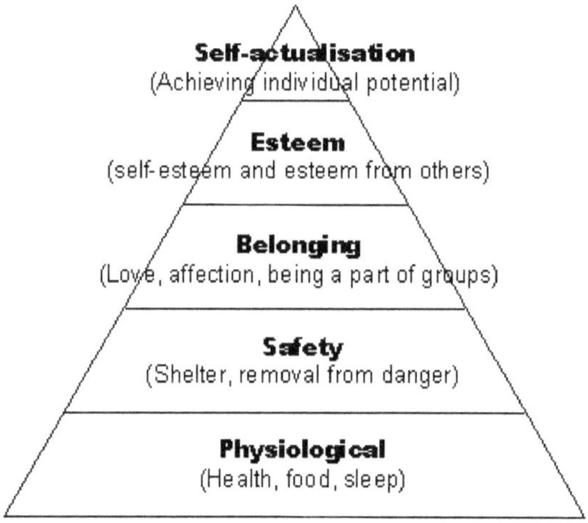

Maslow's Hierarchy of Needs

Maslow believed human behavior is driven by satisfying one's individual needs. In his *Hierarchy of Needs*, he said we are all driven by meeting our lowest level, physical needs first, such as sleep, food and health. Then, once those needs are met, we focus on our safety needs of shelter and preventing danger.

Moving up the pyramid, once we cover the basic needs, we address relational needs, then, work at building our self-esteem. According to Maslow, the highest level of need is reached by the fewest, to achieve individual potential and maximize one's life.

Christian author and psychologist Larry Crabb wrote that we have two types of needs: the need for security and the need for significance.[5] Some people are driven primarily by seeking to be secure. Their focus is on shelter, safety and relationships, similar to Maslow's lower three levels. Others strive to be significant, according to Crabb, having goals of achieving and accomplishing the things they view to be important. These correspond roughly to Maslow's top two levels of needs.

What does your purpose have to do with your needs? We naturally focus on what we believe we need. This focus influences what we believe our purpose in life to be. However, your ultimate purpose needs to be about more than just meeting your own needs. Hold onto this thought, we'll talk about it below.

Exercise 8

Before we go on, let me ask you this: do you want purpose in life? Do you want your life to count for something? Up to this point in your life, what has been your purpose? Write your answer here:

What Kind of Purpose?

Several years ago, millions of people across America witnessed on television the brutal murders of six people in Tucson. They were gathered to talk with Rep. Gabrielle Giffords who was wounded, along with others. 31 bullets shot in 13 quick seconds, resulting in tragedy. I remember thinking, "What a tragic waste of so many lives!"

---

[5] Larry Crabb has several good books, including "Understanding People", "The Marriage Builder" and "Inside Out".

Perhaps you join me in thinking, "what wasted lives," when you think of the millions who languish in prison today, having committed unnecessary, stupid acts, millions more wasting their lives on drugs and alcohol and others wasting their lives by having little or no purpose.

I don't know many people who want no purpose in life, but I do know many who make little effort to discover and live out their purpose. One type of people has no known purpose. They have little direction, little vision for their futures. As Thoreau gloomily wrote, "The mass of men lead lives of quiet desperation."

Worse than dying pre-maturely or struggling to make ends meet is a wasted life. Of all tragedies you might face, living without purpose is one of the worst.

Another type of person has the purpose of self-fulfillment. These people devote their lives to meeting their own needs and wishes. Granted, as humans we all have the desire to meet our basic needs as Maslow explained. However, we need to be careful about only pleasing ourselves. We can literally become addicted to self, becoming increasingly narcissistic. If your focus in life is to serve and please yourself, you will ultimately fail. In my experience, the happiest people in life are those who actively share with others, the unhappiest are those focused on themselves.

I hope you join me in a third group of people, people who choose to live a life of purpose that is bigger than themselves. Max Lucado, a prolific Christian author, stated it well in the title of his book, "Outlive your Life."[6]

---

[6] See "Outlive your Life: You were Made to Make a Difference". Thomas Nelson, 2010.

Your challenge is to rise above simply meeting your own needs, to devote your life to something much bigger than yourself. Imagine living a life that makes a lasting difference, leaving a legacy of enriching others' lives. Even if you never get that 15 minutes of fame, even if most people forget you some day, imagine the joy you will have knowing your life has been worthwhile.

We are called by God to a life of purpose.

God's Purpose for You

When I was a pastor in Europe, we had contact with a Christian music group, Anno Domini, which held concerts for us several times. The lead singer, John Bowers, wrote a song in 1990 called "Something More" that was very moving. He sang, it isn't enough to merely exist, to take care of yourself or to have a few laughs. Somewhere deep down inside, we long for something more.

We may attempt to satisfy this longing by seeking more possessions, more food, more thrills or more feel-good experiences. However, this "something more" goes beyond Maslow's levels of needs. It isn't a need to be fulfilled, rather it is a unique "hole in the soul."

Your purpose begins with a relationship with God. I'm not talking religion, which can be boring and trivial. Rather, it is a relationship that is personal and meaningful, to know Him and to be known by Him, to love Him and to be loved by Him.

This relationship with God is foundational. Your life of purpose should ultimately be shaped by God's purpose for you. His focus is primarily to relate with you, to love and guide and support you. Then, He wants to use you to serve Him, to positively influence the world He has placed you in. The beautiful thing about loving and serving God is this:

As you love and serve God, you will be blessed and your life willed be filled with joy.

Exercise 9

To gain a deeper understanding of His purpose in making you, consider these Scriptures, then fill in the blanks.

For You created my inmost being; You knit me together in my mother's womb.

I praise You because I am fearfully and wonderfully made;
Your works are wonderful, I know that full well. – Ps 139:13-14

I am not an accident. I am _______________________.

For I know the plans I have for you," declares the LORD, "plans to prosper you and not to harm you, plans to give you hope and a future. – Jeremiah 29:11

God has a plan for me, to ________________________.

So do not fear, for I am with you; do not be dismayed,
for I am your God. I will strengthen you and help you;
I will uphold you with My righteous right hand. – Isaiah 41:10

I am not alone, He plans to ______________________.

You did not choose me, but I chose you and appointed you so that you might go and bear fruit—fruit that will last – John 15:16

He chose me to ___________________________.

Give, and it will be given to you. A good measure, pressed down, shaken together and running over, will be poured into your lap. For with the measure you use, it will be measured to you. – Luke 6:38

He promises to ___________ as I _________________.

Summarize what you have learned about God's plan for you:

Discovering your Purpose

Now, let's get more specific. As you consider your purpose in life, it should be based on what God's purpose is for you: that you know Him and walk with Him and serve Him.

It is also based on who you are specifically: how you are wired, your background, your gifts, your interests and your passion. You have unique gifts and abilities that can help you help others. Your history of life experiences can guide you to be more effective in the future. Your personality is unique, too. Use it to help others.

Another part of determining your purpose is to know what others need. If God wants to use you in others' lives, it is important that you recognize what they need. You won't be able to meet all of the needs out there, but you can make a difference in a few. Pray for those in need, pray for wisdom to know where/how you should respond.

Exercise 10

In preparation for this chapter's Life-Changer, there are several things I'd like you to consider. Please answer these questions.

1. Review your values from chapter 8. Summarize them here:

2. Review your history:
   What has God already done for you?

   How has He used you in the past?

3. What is your passion? What do you love? What do you long to do?

4. What needs do you see?

5. What do others think? Seek out some people whose opinions you trust. What do they say your purpose may be?

6. Try something new. You may discover new direction and purpose, if you try something you haven't done before: Volunteer at Habitat for Humanity, read to a child, serve at a soup kitchen, call a hurting friend, write a poem for someone... What could you try?

7. Pray: ask God what He wants you to do, what your purpose should be. "Lord, what do you want of me?"

Gerhard's Story

I met Gerhard at a Christian rock concert in Vienna. On crutches, he came in late and slowly made his way all the way to the front. After the concert, we got to talking and I invited him to the youth group I was leading. As we became better acquainted, he told me his story.

At 16, Gerhard contracted multiple sclerosis, losing his health and most of his friends. As he became more isolated and depressed, he wondered if his life was even worthy of continuing. Then, at 25, his life changed as he met Jesus and began to develop a relationship with God.

The transformation was truly inside-out. God changed him inside, giving him new faith and a new perspective in life. Gerhard went from being depressed and suicidal to being filled with joy and peace, which then began to affect his "outside life." Amazed at the radical transformation in their son, his mother and father both placed their faith in Christ. Then, his brother went from being a skeptic to a believer.

Although his M.S. never improved, Gerhard found purpose in life as he embraced a living relationship with God and shared his joy with others. Over the next years, Gerhard made a difference in dozens of young people who learned joy in life isn't dependent on life's circumstances. In spite of his handicap, Gerhard lived out God's purpose for him by giving others hope and joy.

Life-Changer #9 Your Life-Purpose Statement.

Where there is no vision, the people perish. – Proverbs 29:18 (KJV)

Just like the Pilgrims, it is important to have a clear vision, or purpose. It will guide you as you grow and change in life. One way to be clear on your purpose is to write a life-purpose statement. Millions of people have benefitted from having a short life-purpose statement. It is a standard tool for life-coaching and for life-planning.

I have carried my life-purpose statement in my Bible for years. I often re-read it and sometimes change it a bit. It reminds me what my life is really about, what is really important. Sometimes, it corrects me, warning me to get back on course, to not go down a "bunny trail." It always encourages me, giving me strength to persevere and live for God and others.

Steps to develop your Life-Purpose Statement:

1. Review your work in Exercise 10. Circle the thoughts/ideas that are most important to you.
2. Use bullet-points to make a list of the key components of your life-purpose:
   -
   -
   -
   -
   -

3. Write your Life-Purpose Statement here. Either use the bullets or write yourself a short letter or whatever works for you.

4. Write out your Life-Purpose Statement again on a separate piece of paper. Keep it somewhere you will see if often: on your desk, in your Bible, on the fridge… Read it every day this week, pray over it, make it yours…

FOCUS — Read. Reflect. Pray. Do.

Psalm 51:10-12

Create in me a pure heart, O God, and renew a steadfast spirit within me. Do not cast me from Your presence or take Your Holy Spirit from me. Restore to me the joy of Your salvation and grant me a willing spirit, to sustain me.

What is the main point of the passage?

How does it apply to me?

My Challenge Today

What challenges / opportunities await me today?

How do I want to respond to them?

My Focus Today

What is my guiding thought for today?

My Prayer Today

Specific things I am trusting God for:

For Further Study this Week

Luke 6:38, Jeremiah 29:11, John 15:9-17, John 15:18-16:4, John 16:5-16, John 16:17-33

10 Choosing a Life of Integrity

A man stopped by the local KFC to pick up chicken dinners for a picnic with his date. At the park, when he and the young lady opened the bag, they discovered something else besides chicken and mashed potatoes. The KFC worker had inadvertently put their food in with the day's receipts, over $800. Surprised, the picnicker did something most people don't do. He drove right back to KFC and presented the money to the manager. Overjoyed at getting the $800 back, the manager exclaimed "We'll call the newspaper and have your picture in the paper!" To this the picnicker replied, "No! Don't do that...you see, the lady I am with isn't my wife...she is someone else's wife."[7]

> *He who is faithful in a very little thing is faithful also in much; and he who is unrighteous in a very little thing is unrighteous also in much. - Luke 16:10*

Why do we agree that integrity is fundamental to a successful life, but we don't want to be bothered by it when it becomes inconvenient? We easily pay lip-service to integrity and we want to be honest and dependable, yet living a life of integrity can be hard work. It is hard to be honest and consistent. It is much easier to quickly ignore our inconsistencies or lies when the truth is uncomfortable.

It's been said,

> *Integrity is like a bag of peanuts, everyone wants some as long as it doesn't cost too much.*

---

[7] Charles Swindoll, Growing Deep in the Christian Life, p. 159-60.

What is Integrity?

Integrity can formally be defined as adherence to moral and ethical principles. It is sound moral character based on honesty and consistency of values and actions. Specialists in ethics tell us integrity requires congruency, meaning a person's words and actions match the values you embrace.

The opposite of integrity is hypocrisy. I don't know anyone who wants to be labeled a hypocrite. In fact, being a hypocrite is one of society's taboos, something to be feared and avoided. It is almost like being called a bigot. You don't want to be known as either. However, do people fear *being* a hypocrite as much as being *called* a hypocrite? If they did, they might live with more integrity.

A fifth-grade teacher posted her class's definition of integrity on the internet: doing the right thing, even when no one else is watching. If you have integrity in life, you are honest and consistent and you can be counted on to "practice what you preach."

There is a subtle difference between integrity and honesty. Honesty means telling the truth, regardless of what you've done, good or bad. Integrity is based on honesty but expands to include more; you consistently adhere to your values or moral code, rejecting things you feel would break your code.

Why Integrity is So Important

Most people agree integrity is absolutely essential for society. Imagine a football game where there are no sidelines, no boundaries to contain the game. There would be chaos without the rules being enforced. Perhaps the next step would be for players to bring weapons onto the expanded field?

In the same way, society doesn't function without people living honestly and consistently with one another. Integrity is needed in every government, in every relationship, in every family and in every marriage.

Without it, we hopelessly self-destruct into little islands of self-interest and mistrust.

That is precisely the point! We agree that we must have integrity to survive and succeed. Indeed, honesty and consistent fairness is foundational to our society and to every relationship. Yet, if we are completely honest, don't we want *others* to *always* be people of integrity...and don't *we* want to be people of integrity, *most* of the time? We have the tempting desire to be the exception to the rule, to not get too specific when it regards ourselves.

For this reason, integrity has to be one of the Four Life Priorities, along with purpose, quality and love. Integrity is fundamental to a successful life, essential to the lasting life change we are working on in *Keep the Change!*

> *Somebody once said that in looking for people to hire, you look for three qualities: integrity, intelligence, and energy. And if they don't have the first, the other two will kill you.*
> *— Warren Buffett*

The Benefits of Integrity

When you live out integrity, you are freed up from many struggles. You won't have to worry about being ridiculed or rejected by others; you focus on doing what you believe to be right. By clinging to the truth you won't have to juggle the lies, what you said to whom. You will be freed from having to inflate the truth to impress others. You no longer try to be someone you really aren't. Rather, when you are committed to truth, they will either accept you as-is or they won't. Either way, you will be freed from pretending.

You will know God accepts you just as you are; you are okay. You will no longer have to perform for or impress others.

By choosing integrity, you are choosing the path of godliness. Since God is truth and can always be counted on, when you strive for integrity, you are seeking to become more like Him (John 3:33, Galatians 5:22-23, Philippians 3:8). As you live out integrity, you become a beacon of God's light and give glory to your Creator.

Think of the impact integrity has in your personal life. If your child or partner can't count on you, there will be no trust. Without trust, you can't have true intimacy or bonding. However, if you are honest and dependable, your family and friends will rely on you and on your word. Your consistency will help lay the foundation for strong interpersonal relationships. Remember the power of your example in your children, as Harry Chapin reminded us in his famous, 1974 "Cat's in the Cradle" ballad,

I'm gonna be like you, dad. You know I'm gonna be like you.

Your children will follow your good or bad example. If you want your children to succeed in life, choose a lifestyle of integrity you want them to emulate.

Also, consider the benefits of living with integrity. You will build a reputation of honesty and trustworthiness. Others will know you can be counted on. Even if you get no nationwide attention for your dependability, it is important. In many careers, having such a reputation is central to success. For example, many sales seminars stress the value of the salesman being known for honesty and dependability.

Integrity is Tough

All of this is not to imply that living a life of integrity is easy. Think of the challenges we face. In a world where integrity is expected, it seems everyone else cheats. In some circles of society, cheating is the norm. Consider these statistics:

- More than 50% of university students in Canada cheat.[8]
- 16% of Americans underreport their earnings at tax time.[9]
- 25% of all search engine requests are for pornography.[10]
- 90% of Americans believe adultery is morally wrong; yet, over 32% of men and 14% of women have committed adultery at least once.[11]

A well-known car dealer in Phoenix has the reputation that he wants to sell everyone in the Valley a car once. Reportedly, his intent is to maximize his profit so much, he doesn't care if the customer feels cheated and never comes back.

With the backdrop of "everyone else is doing it," it is easy for us to yield to the temptation to shade the truth, to promise what we can't deliver and to fudge the numbers. How simple just to join in, since "no one will ever know."

---

[8] Gulli, Kohler and Patriquin, "The great university cheating scandal." Macleans.ca, Feb.9, 2007.

[9] Denise Chow, "Why we cheat on our taxes." www.MSNBC.com, April 14, 2010.

[10] See Infidelity statistics, www.womansavers.com.

[11] See www.womansavers.com and www.infidelityman.com.

Psalm 73 – Words about Integrity

Another response to hypocrisy we may choose is to bemoan the unfairness of it all. This reminds me of what Asaph wrote about the "wicked":

> *For I envied the arrogant when I saw the prosperity of the wicked.*
> *They have no struggles; their bodies are healthy and strong.*
> *They are free from common human burdens; they are not plagued by human ills. – Psalm 73:3-5*

Over 3000 years ago, this psalmist felt much the way we may feel: frustrated, resentful, angry...and tempted to join in. He went on to write:

> *From their callous hearts comes iniquity; their evil imaginations have no limits. They scoff and speak with malice; with arrogance they threaten oppression. Surely in vain I have kept my heart pure and have washed my hands in innocence. – Psalm 73:7-8,13*

Do you hear him complaining to God how unfair it is? "Why does everything go so smoothly for the bad guys, while the good guys struggle just to get by?" I remember one gloomy day when I sat in the parking lot of the local Costco and watched all of the wealthy people unload their overflowing carts of trinkets into their BMW's and Cadillacs. I cried out to God, "Unfair! Why do they…" I sounded just like Asaph!

Fortunately, God had something to say to Asaph, to me and to all of us:

> *When I tried to understand all this, it troubled me deeply till I entered the sanctuary of God; then I understood their final destiny.*
> *Surely You place them on slippery ground; You cast them down to ruin. – Psalm 73:16-18*

God tells us He knows what is going on. He watches over all, the righteous and the unrighteous. What goes around comes around. He hasn't forgotten your faithfulness nor has He forgotten others as they selfishly treat others unfairly. Yet, don't put your focus on the bad guys "getting their just desserts." If you do, it will consume you and take your focus off living for God.

> *When my heart was grieved and my spirit embittered, I was senseless and ignorant; I was a brute beast before you. – Psalm 73:21-22*

Don't worry about whether others are hypocrites or cheaters. That is God's job. Your job is to turn back to Him, to live for Him and to embrace integrity, keeping a healthy perspective about what is really important.

> *But as for me, it is good to be near God. Whom have I in heaven but You? And earth has nothing I desire besides You. My flesh and my heart may fail, but God is the strength of my heart and my portion forever. – Psalm 73:25-26,28*

How to Embrace Integrity

If the temptations are so real and integrity is so hard to maintain, who can possibly do it? Why not join the hypocrites or give up? Here is the essential point: you can't do it on your own. Yes, you have many choices to make, but you will ultimately need God's help to become a man or woman of integrity.

In Luke 19:1-10, Zaccheus was a wealthy tax collector who was universally hated. When Jesus called him down from his perch in a tree, he must have wondered why Christ would want to speak with him. Would He condemn him? Reject him? Talk down to him? That's what I think I would do with such a bad guy who made his wealth by cheating his own people.

Instead, Jesus invited the taxman to dinner and began a relationship with him. As he experienced acceptance and forgiveness, Zaccheus embraced his new relationship with Christ. Then, he admitted to and turned from his unethical practices (repentance). He also sought restoration with those he had injured.

Zaccheus became a man of integrity. This can also be your pattern for a life of integrity. Here it is in a nutshell:

1. See your need; you are powerless to live a life of integrity on your own strength.

2. Meet Jesus: don't settle for religion, plug into an exciting relationship with the Son of God.

3. Admit hypocrisy: none of us measures up to integrity. Identify specifically where you fall short. Don't rationalize or make excuses.

4. Choose to live with integrity today. Start with one area that you can change: stop the lies; don't ask your kids to do something you aren't doing; read your Bible and pray daily; practice what you preach…

5. Restore: look for something you need to "make right." Correct a wrong, seek forgiveness…do something this week to make amends.

When Kent Keith was 19 and a student at Harvard, he first wrote the Paradoxical Commandments as a booklet for high school student leaders he was working with.

Only 30,000 copies were originally published, but they have since been read by millions. A copy was even found hanging in Mother Teresa's room. They call us to higher ethical living. Join me in choosing a life of integrity.

The Paradoxical Commandments

People are illogical, unreasonable, and self-centered.
Love them anyway.

If you do good, people will accuse you of selfish ulterior motives.
Do good anyway.

If you are successful, you win false friends and true enemies.
Succeed anyway.

The good you do today will be forgotten tomorrow.
Do good anyway.

Honesty and frankness make you vulnerable.
Be honest and frank anyway.

The biggest men and women with the biggest ideas can be
shot down by the smallest men and women with the smallest minds.
Think big anyway.

People favor underdogs but follow only top dogs.
Fight for a few underdogs anyway.

What you spend years building may be destroyed overnight.
Build anyway.

People really need help but may attack you if you do help them.
Help people anyway.

Give the world the best you have and you'll get kicked in the teeth.
Give the world the best you have anyway.

Kent Keith, 1968. www.paradoxicalcommandments.com

Life-Changer #10 Embrace Integrity in your Life

This exercise should help you turn your desire for integrity into reality, to better "practice what you preach."

1. Express your need for integrity. Write a note to God and to yourself, admitting your lack of integrity and that you can't do it on your own strength.

   I can't do this by myself. I need…

2. Meet Jesus: renew your relationship with Jesus. Take some time with God. Read Luke 19:1-10. Listen to Him; talk to Him.

3. Admit hypocrisy:

   I am sometimes a hypocrite. I have…

4. Choose to live with integrity today. Start with one area that you can change:

   What should I change?

   What should I start doing differently?

   Where should I "practice what I preach?"

5. Restore: what do I need to "make right?"

   What do I need to correct?

   Whose forgiveness do I need to seek?

Focus — Read. Reflect. Pray. Do.

Psalm 73:21-24

> *When my heart was grieved and my spirit embittered, I was senseless and ignorant; I was a brute beast before You. Yet I am always with You; You hold me by my right hand. You guide me with Your counsel, and afterward You will take me into glory.*

What is the main point of the passage?

How does it apply to me?

My Challenge Today

What challenges / opportunities await me today?

How do I want to respond to them?

My Focus Today

What is my guiding thought for today?

My Prayer Today

Specific things I am trusting God for:

For Further Study this Week

John 17:1-19, John 17:20-25, John 18:1-11, John 18:12-27, John 18:28-40, John 19:1-16

11 The Quest for Quality

I think everyone has a story about something made of cheap quality. You purchased that item at the discount store, came home to use it and the crazy thing broke, on the very first time! How maddening! When something is brand new, it should work as intended, right? Sure, we all know "you get what you pay for" and "you can always take it back," but don't you expect a certain minimal level of quality? Of course you do.

> *The quality of a person's life is in direct proportion to their commitment to excellence, regardless of their chosen field of endeavor.*
>
> - Vince Lombardi, NFL Coach

We not only expect quality in our merchandise, we expect good quality in most things in life. We want our cars to run properly, our children to get a quality education and our restaurants to use food of good quality. We also want businesses to use quality in their customer service, our healthcare to be professional and our airlines to maintain good quality in their planes. Do these expectations seem reasonable to you? Absolutely! Our society is built around such demands for quality.

As necessary as good quality is, I am amazed at how easily we allow the quality to drop. Not only is there less quality in many aspects of our life today, we are literally failing to maintain high quality in essential areas of life. Consider education: U.S. high school students routinely rank in the lowest third of developed nations for math, far behind the countries of Western Europe (Wall Street Journal, Dec.6, 2010).

Naturally, it is easier to expect quality and to promise quality than it is to deliver quality. However, the lack of quality we face today is profound. This dearth of excellence isn't just on the corporate or professional level, it is especially lacking on the personal level.

Today, I invite you to join me in a quest for quality, to not merely complain about poor workmanship and failing schools. Instead, I invite you to personally join me in making a lasting difference by developing a lifestyle of quality, to not only choose quality because it is smart business, but to live out quality as an expression of whom you want to be.

What is Quality?

Quality is sometimes more easily identified by what it isn't. Quality isn't shoddy workmanship or poor service. It isn't achieved by a laissez-faire, easy-going-bordering-on-lazy work ethic; rather, it involves deliberately seeking to do your best.

As Henry Ford said,

> *Quality means doing it right when no one is looking.*

I lived in central Europe for 10 years, where I observed the quality of home construction. While most American homes were built in three to four months, as cheaply as possible, Europeans built their homes to last for many generations. Even the rain gutters were of high quality. My neighbor put copper gutters on his home, so his grandchildren wouldn't have to worry about re-doing the gutters in 60 years. His home was "built to last."[12]

---

[12] See *Built to Last*, Collins and Porras, 1974: an interesting discussion about American companies that have a long-range vision embracing high quality products and services.

Star-caliber athletes achieve their great performance by relentlessly pursuing quality. Green Bay Packers coaching legend Vince Lombardi was known for his focus on flawless performance of the basics. UCLA basketball coach John Wooden developed his Pyramid of Success, stating

> *Success is peace of mind, which is a direct result of self-satisfaction in knowing you made the effort to do your best to become the best that you are capable of becoming.*[13]

Quality can be developed, if it is a high priority. In the 1970's, Honda was known by Americans to make cheap, little cars that rusted out quickly. The good gas mileage these cars offered didn't outweigh their shortcomings, until two things happened: gas became more expensive and Honda improved its quality. In less than 25 years, Honda vehicles became known as some of the most dependable cars! Millions of them are sold each year, even though other brands are cheaper. People are starved for quality!

Being committed to quality doesn't mean perfectionism, instead it is a commitment to excellence. What is the difference? Perfectionism can't accept any mistakes or flaws. Everything must be perfect, regardless of the financial or human cost. In contrast, excellence is doing your best with the resources (time, money, materials, manpower, know-how) you have available.

People who are perfectionists can be very difficult to get along with. Their standards for themselves and others are often unreasonably high, because they are trying to achieve perfection. However, when you are committed to high quality, or to excellence, there is still room for "grace" in dealing with other people. You try to do your best and encourage others to do

---

[13] See The Wooden Course, www.woodencourse.com

so also, but, if the result isn't perfection, you gracefully accept it. You recognize that the people involved are as important as the product.

Sports psychologist Terry Orlick first published his influential book, *The Pursuit of Excellence*, in 1980. He challenged people from all walks of life to envision and commit to excellence. Orlick writes of the "wheel of excellence" which includes six key elements (confidence, distraction control, on-going learning, commitment, mental readiness, positive images). These elements form the perimeter of the wheel which revolves around the seventh, central element: focus.[14]

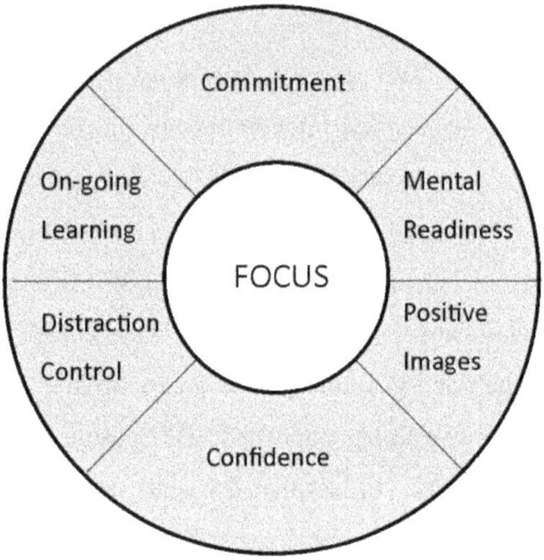

Orlick's Wheel of Excellence

Excellence is not something we attain, it is a goal we continuously pursue. Committing to high quality isn't a destination, it is a lifestyle.

Quality is not an act, it is a habit. – Aristotle

As I write this, I'm enjoying a cup of Earl Grey tea at a popular local café. People line up for coffee and tea. They come in suits, heels, jeans and shorts. They come alone, meet a friend or study partner or have a Bridge club gathering. Why do they come here? Why do they line up to pay $2-5 for a

---

[14] *The Pursuit of Excellence*, Orlick, Human Kinetics, 1980.

beverage? The answer, in part, is quality. People can count on good service. They can count on good products. They come for the quality.

Why Commit to Quality?

God Himself set the standard for quality. After the third, fourth, fifth and sixth days of creation, "God saw all that he had made, and it was very good" (Genesis 1:6-31).

One of the examples of quality in the Old Testament was the detail and care that was to go into building the temple. Many chapters of Leviticus are devoted to instructing the Jewish people how to construct and maintain this central place of worship. Constructed with large amounts of gold, silver and precious stones, the temple was a theological symbol for the value and centrality of worshipping God (Leviticus 27). Quality was an expression of the perfection of God Himself.

As God's Son, Jesus continued in this godly expression of quality in everything He did. Mark's gospel writes of Him,

> *People were overwhelmed with amazement. "He has done everything well," they said. "He even makes the deaf hear and the mute speak."* – Mark 7:37.

As followers of Christ, Christians are called to be modern-day temples.

> *Don't you know that you yourselves are God's temple and that God's Spirit dwells in your midst? ...God's temple is sacred, and you together are that temple.* – 1 Corinthians 3:16-17.

Your life can be a living temple where God is worshipped. By committing to a life of quality, you literally can give Him glory and, at the same time, enjoy the benefits of a quality life.

To achieve quality on the outside, you need to think quality and live quality on the inside. It is a quest you begin and continue long-term. Even if you don't immediately see results, you have the satisfaction and the peace of mind that you are living for the Lord, and, that your pursuit of excellence will pay off. I like business columnist and motivational speaker Harvey Mackay's story about growing bamboo. Once a bamboo seed is planted, the farmer waters it daily for four years with no visible results. Then, the bamboo grows 60 feet in the next 90 days! (www.earlytorise.com , Sept. 7, 2010)

The quality, not the longevity, of one's life is what is important.
– Martin Luther King, Jr.

Chuck is a friend of mine who exudes quality. When we first met through sailing, I noticed Chuck's boat was not only neat and tidy, but also well maintained. Good boat maintenance is a big safety factor. When calamity hits on the water, it's important to know your equipment will perform well.

As a tax accountant, his livelihood depends on getting the details right. He doesn't have to advertise his business because his satisfied customers spread the word to their friends. Even in a down economy, Chuck's tax business has grown every year. Although not perfect as a person, he can be counted on. He arrives to appointments on-time. People are always glad to see Chuck's smile on his face and to enjoy his upbeat attitude. Quality counts for Chuck.

It's been often said, "a life worth living is a life worth living well." As you review how your life fits with a life of quality, I encourage you to not settle for less. Don't accept the status quo or what others expect of you. For your life, think outside the box. Refuse to be limited by excuses or shallow thinking. You aren't alone on this journey. Many others join you in seeking to be the best they can be. They know God Himself will support them as they seek to honor them with their work, their relationships, their thinking and their character.

Life-Changer #11 My Quest for Quality

1. Summarize what you have learned from this chapter:

2. Evaluate these areas of your life for quality:
   (check which column applies)

	needs improvement	am doing well
Career		
Care of possessions (car, house…)		
Relationship with spouse		
Relationship with children		
Relationship with God		
Service to others		

3. What specifically do you need to improve on?

4. Choose one area to begin to change today:

   I want to improve quality in …

   I will begin by…

FOCUS — Read. Reflect. Pray. Do.

Psalm 73:25-28

Whom have I in heaven but You? And earth has nothing I desire besides You. My flesh and my heart may fail, but God is the strength of my heart and my portion forever. Those who are far from You will perish; You destroy all who are unfaithful to You.
But as for me, it is good to be near God. I have made the Sovereign LORD my refuge; I will tell of all Your deeds.

What is the main point of the passage?

How does it apply to me?

My Challenge Today

What challenges / opportunities await me today?

How do I want to respond to them?

My Focus Today

What is my guiding thought for today?

My Prayer Today

Specific things I am trusting God for:

For Further Study this Week

Mark 7:31-37, 1 Cor. 3:16-17, John 19:17-27, John 19:30-20:9, John 20:20-23, John 20:24-30

12 Living for Love

In preparing to write this chapter, I've been thinking and reflecting on love for several days. I find myself confused. Why is it that so much is written about love, so much is sung about love, so many movies have the theme of love and yet, we don't seem to be very good at it?[15] Do you know anyone who is an expert at love?

> *As I have loved you…love one another.* – Jesus, John 13:34

"Well", you may respond, "what are we talking about? Are we talking about a romantic feeling, sex, a kind gesture, loving 'that new outfit'…or what?" That is part of the problem. We use the term love to mean several different things. For a moment, though, let's zero in on a non-romantic, selfless form of love.

It's safe to say almost everyone wants to be loved. We know how it feels to be unloved, that painful feeling of rejection or of being ignored. We hurt when friends or family members don't value us. Naturally, we want to avoid that and, instead, experience the warmth and care from another human. We want to be accepted, to be treated with kindness. We want to be loved.

In spite of our culture, in spite of what runs our economy, in spite of frantic lifestyles, people are hungry for love. Our society rewards numbers (wealth, performance…), status, notoriety, popularity; but, we have a deeper need to be accepted and loved. Even though kindness is rarely noticed by the

---

[15] Consider these big hit songs and the vocalists who made them famous: "What the world needs now is love, sweet love"(Jackie DeShannon,1965), "All you need is love"(John Lennon, 1967), "What's love got to do with it?"(Tina Turner, 1993).

media, we all want it. In the midst of an increasingly isolated lifestyle, where we are overworked, overstressed and overextended, we long for personal attention and touch.

Is love like a Christmas gift? Are we better at receiving it than at giving it? Certainly, it is human nature to focus on ourselves, to think more about what we get than about what we give to someone else. Maybe that's why most of us aren't great at loving others, because it is too easy to stay focused on ourselves. Or, we give conditionally, we only give love when we believe we will receive something in return.

If I were to ask you, "How is your love life?"...you might be offended that I was being a bit too nosy. But, let me ask anyway, how is your love life?

Exercise 11

How are you doing at loving those God has brought into your life? Take a moment to reflect and write your answer here:

I began this chapter with the focus on how most of us aren't very good at loving others, but I'm sure you can think of some people who break the mold, people who are good at loving. Throughout this book, I've given you examples of everyday people who personified the subject we are looking at. Now, it's time for you to help us out.

Exercise 12

What is the best example of love you can think of? Who is the most loving person you know? Why is he/she so good at loving others?

Pete Brady of Brookfield, Connecticut is a great example of someone who loves people. Several years ago, he noticed the many elderly people in his community having trouble raking their leaves and maintaining their homes. Pete wasn't especially handy, but he could rake leaves. He started helping seniors. He was also a good organizer, so he got other volunteers involved. They raked leaves, painted walls and did a variety of odd jobs for people who needed a little help. Because Pete saw a need and was willing to express love, Brookfield now has dozens of volunteers helping hundreds of needy people every year (www.msnbc.com/nightlynews, Making a Difference, Dec.10, 2010.

Love Defined

As noted before, in English we understand love to mean several different things. We know about romantic and passionate love (eros). We also have the concept of brotherly love (phileo) and the godly, non-selfish, unconditional type of love (agape). These 3 Greek terms eros, phileo and agape are New Testament concepts.

For many, love is transactional or conditional. We give love so we can get something in return. If we don't receive back something of value, a hug or a thank-you or a similar expression of love, we'll stop giving out love. This conditional form of loving is extremely natural and common; yet, by attaching conditions, don't we really make it less about love and more about getting what we want? Conditional love invariably leads to performance-pressure and irritation, disappointment and anger when we don't get or give what was expected.

Let's return to God's form of unconditional love, agape. The noun, *agape*, and verb, *agapao*, appear throughout the New Testament and describe God's love: how the Father loves the Son, how He loves people and how His followers are called to adopt this type of love for one another. The clearest example of God's love is found in John 3:16:

> *For God so loved the world that He gave His one and only Son, that whoever believes in Him shall not perish but have eternal life.*

In this simple passage, Jesus expressed several profound concepts:

1. God's love is both feeling and action. He *loved* so much that He *gave*. He backed up emotion with deed. If you love someone, you care enough to act on it.

2. God's love is limitless. He didn't limit love to the "good guys." His love is for all who believe.

3. God's love is precious. He gave His only Son for us.

4. God's love is purposeful. There was a reason for Christ's sacrifice: our sin.

5. God's love is unconditional. It is a gift. He gets nothing in return.

God's type of love can require significant sacrifice or cost to the one doing the loving. Consider this:

> *Greater love has no one than this: to lay down one's life for one's friends.* John 15:13

Jesus gave up His rights and His life for us. As we seek to love others, we need to be prepared to love sacrificially. You may not need to die for someone like Jesus did. Rather, you may be called to live for others, as Paul wrote:

> *Therefore, I urge you, brothers and sisters, in view of God's mercy, to offer your bodies as a living sacrifice, holy and pleasing to God—this is your true and proper worship.* – Romans 12:1

This brings us to a working definition of the love we so desperately need to experience and to share with others.

> *This form of love is a generous, selfless expression of kindness and care, seeking to help or encourage someone else.*

Yesterday, I received an email from Don and Sherry, a soft-spoken, retired couple who know about love. Fifty years ago, they were moved by God's love and decided to do what they could to share it with others. Packing up their belongings and their four children, they boarded a ship and spent the next thirty years on the mission field sharing God's love. Often misunderstood, sometimes ridiculed, they overcame loneliness and language barriers to encourage new believers in their faith. Don and Sherry chose to love God and others by devoting their lives to service. Because of their loving actions, hundreds, or perhaps thousands, were touched by God's love.

Love Enabled

There is naturally great risk involved in selfless loving. You may wonder, "Who is going to take care of me?" You don't know for sure that others will respond to your love by giving back to you. You could give and give to others…and receive little or nothing in return. Unconditional loving requires a leap of faith, doesn't it?

Here is Jesus' promise which your leap of faith can be based on:

Give and it will be given to you. A good measure, pressed down, shaken together and running over, will be poured into your lap. For with the measure you use, it will be measured to you. – Luke 6:38

This is the central question: do you believe God is able to take care of you? If you choose to extend yourself and generously give love to others, to not keep track of what you may get in return and not hold back, do you believe God will provide for your needs?

Exercise 13

Do you believe God is able to take care of you, if you reach out in love to others? Your answer to this question is pivotal. Write your answer here:

Our human nature tells us to not risk getting involved with others, to hold back resources and just take care of ourselves. We are tempted to focus on ourselves, to be selfish. In the past 37 years of ministry, I've had the privilege of working with thousands of people from all walks of life representing dozens of countries and cultures. One thing has become clear to me: selfish people are unhappy; generous, loving people are much happier in life. It's true!

Amassing wealth won't satisfy your longings. Solely taking care of yourself will only make you miserable. We are happiest and most well-adjusted in life when we are actively giving to and caring for others.

How do we overcome our selfishness? Our need for greed? Our focus on ourselves? Frankly, we can't do it on our own. You and I can make daily choices to love, but we ultimately won't succeed on our own power. Just like everything else we've addressed in this book, we need God's help in changing our lives, we need His strength to love Him and others.

We love because He first loved us. – 1 John 4:19

By plugging into and experiencing God's love personally, you will gain the strength to love others. Wait a moment. Before you move on, stop and consider this. Even though you've heard this many times before, let me ask: has God's love impacted you?

Deep down in your soul, do you get how big a deal this is?

You are accepted. You are forgiven. You are valued. You are loved.

Scot Lewis of Mahoning County, Ohio found a way to show others God's love. In his part of the state, he noticed how many rural families were struggling to feed themselves. They didn't have access to the services commonly found in the cities. Together with his church, Scot decided to do something about the need. They started gathering and giving away food to needy people. Several years later, the Big Reach Center of Hope is the second-largest food bank in Ohio, feeding thousands of people every month. Scot chose to love others (Christianity Today, Jan. 2011).

Love Applied

When you mimic God's version of love, you not only follow in His ways, you are changed. By simply loving others with no expectation of receiving anything in return, you are set free.

No longer are your relationships based on performance. You don't have to meet others' needs to be accepted and you don't need them to meet your needs or wishes. Rather, your focus is on helping, accepting and encouraging others. You become free as never before.

Many of us can be pretty good at loving others outside of the home. We volunteer, we help little old ladies or we politely hold the door for the next person. During your lunch hour, you may politely listen to someone at work who needs attention. However, the biggest challenge most of us face in loving others is at home.

> *How you treat your partner, your children or other family members is the true measure of your love.*

Barbara and I have often asked ourselves the question, "Why do we treat the people we love the most, the worst?" Why do we blow up in anger at our family, anger that we'd never display somewhere else? Would you raise your voice at the store clerk like you do with your spouse?

There are certainly some explanations for this. We expect more from our partners than we do from the store clerk. We lower our guard at home, while most of us are on good behavior out in public. We may be tired at the end of the day when we get home and are, therefore, more irritable.

However, it goes deeper than this. You have history with your family members. There are established patterns of relating that have gone on for years. Also, your family sees the real "you" and you see the real "them."

The challenge of love is to love someone in spite of the history and the past patterns. Your challenge is to forgive the past hurts and intentionally love those people God has brought into your life.

Dani faced the biggest challenge in her life when her 17 year-old daughter, Casey, ran away from home. For six months, Dani didn't know where she was, other than to hear rumors of Casey living on the streets of Phoenix. After beating herself up for months, Dani struggled to get past her hurt and anger. She chose to forgive her daughter, even though she hadn't returned or asked for forgiveness. Dani prepared herself to love her daughter unconditionally, if she ever got the chance. The beautiful end to this story: within a week, Dani got her chance when Casey returned home. Like the Prodigal Son's father, Dani didn't rant and rave; instead, she welcomed her daughter home. Dani's act of selfless love paved the way for Casey to not only come home, but to repent of her mistakes and rebuild her relationship with her mother.

When you choose to love as God has loved you, amazing things can happen. Join me in living out the love God has given us.

Life-Changer #12 Living for Love

1. Summarize what you have learned from this chapter:

2. What would your life be like if you were deeply aware of God's love for you every day?

3. What would your life be like if you chose to show God's love to others every day?

4. What would your family be like if you chose to show them God's love every day?

5. Where do you need to start?

   Who needs your love?

   What can you do?

Focus — Read. Reflect. Pray. Do.

Psalm 103:1-5

Praise the LORD, my soul; all my inmost being, praise His holy name. Praise the LORD, my soul, and forget not all His benefits— who forgives all your sins and heals all your diseases, who redeems your life from the pit and crowns you with love and compassion, who satisfies your desires with good things so that your youth is renewed like the eagle's.

What is the main point of the passage?

How does it apply to me?

My Challenge Today

What challenges / opportunities await me today?

How do I want to respond to them?

My Focus Today

What is my guiding thought for today?

My Prayer Today

Specific things I am trusting God for:

For Further Study this Week

1 John 4:19, Luke 6:38, Luke 24:1-12, Luke 24:13-53,
John 21;1-14, Acts 1:1-11,

13 The Harmony of Life

Harmony is the active process of understanding and living at peace: peace with yourself, with your world, with the people in your life.

Recently, I've spoken with a number of people about harmony: harmony in music, harmony in life, harmony at home... I've spoken with musicians, pastors and everyday people. As we've talked, I remembered an incident from my high school.

> *But what is happiness except the simple harmony between a man and the life he leads?*
>
> *- Albert Camus*

When I was an aspiring trombonist in the Princeton High School band, our band director, Mr. Lueck, suddenly stepped down from the podium and hid behind a music stand. While most of the band stopped playing, one boy playing the trumpet kept on playing, oblivious to the band director. Mr. Lueck then waived his hands and his baton while the trumpeter kept blaring slightly off-key notes. Finally, the director launched his baton at the unsuspecting trumpeter, bringing the sour sounds to an end! Everyone else smiled. No sound at all was better than sour sounds.

Whether you enjoy country or classical, rap or rock, jazz or swing, everyone loves good music. We may disagree on styles of music and on what volume is best, but most of us enjoy hearing the melodies and harmonies produced by gifted musicians. These artists work together to blend tones and rhythms into pleasing beauty for the ear.

We enjoy harmonies that complement the melodies. Whether it is the Three Tenors, Christine and the Phantom, or the Messiah, the harmony is central to the experience. Rather than hearing only a soloist, we value how the musicians weave their instruments and voices together. They practice many hours to achieve excellence and beauty.

In contrast to harmony, disharmony gives us the feeling of dissonance and confusion. Whether in music or in life, we don't like disharmony. It is frustrating, sometimes painful and often appears to be wasted effort and time. Disharmony comes easily with little effort, while harmony is purposeful and requires intentionality. Harmony demands hard work, but is worth the effort. This leads us to ask, what is harmony, how does it apply to us and how do we make it work?

Understanding Harmony

From the world of music, a good harmony has several key components:

- Pay attention — the musician follows the director and is aware what other musicians are doing
- Express self — the musician plays or sings, using his gifts
- Work together — cooperation is essential, musicians are on "the same page"
- Practice! — being gifted isn't enough, the serious musician practices his craft
- Enjoy together — music should be fun, worthwhile

Similar to a musician, we need harmony in life. We need to pay attention to our lives, to be self-aware. We need to express ourselves well, using the gifts and strengths God has given us. We need the different aspects of life to work together or we fall into disharmony. If we don't immediately succeed, we keep practicing to get better at harmony. Finally, we need to enjoy the life He has given, which is only possible when we weave life together in harmony.

You may never think about harmonizing your life. This may even sound a bit far-fetched, that you can't possibly control life and that you aren't the director waving the baton. I fully agree. You aren't the band director of life. You don't control whether you it snows or whether you get cancer or whether you win the lottery. You aren't God.

> *Harmony is the active process of understanding and living at peace: peace with yourself, with your world, with the people in your life.*

However, God gives us a great deal of freedom and responsibility in life. There are many choices you and I make. We choose whether to exercise or watch TV. We choose how to respond to our daughters when they misbehave. We choose whether to read the Bible or Sporting News or Cosmopolitan.

Sadly, some people believe they don't have many choices in life, that all is pre-determined. They feel they might as well give up, resulting in apathy and complaints. This understanding of life doesn't square with God's plan for us. Jesus told us,

> *I came that they may have life, and have it abundantly.* – John 10:10

God has always intended for us to enjoy life, now and for eternity. He knows we will best enjoy our lives when we follow His leadership and choose to obey and love.

Let's go back to the band director analogy. Consider that God is your director. He chooses the music and waives the baton and indicates which section of instruments should play when and how loudly. Think of yourself as the lead trumpeter, first chair of the trumpet section. The trumpets are the different components of your life. You have the responsibility to follow, to stay in touch with the director and to play your part. You also are responsible for your section of trumpets, the various aspects of your life. You work with them, you coordinate with them and you enjoy making music with them.

As she entered her 50's, Sandy noticed her metabolism was changing. Each year she had a little less energy and a few more pounds. Not only did this affect her physically, it also affected how she felt about herself and her relationships. She smiled less and "grumped" more. She felt "off" just a bit, out of harmony with herself and others.

While these body changes are natural, they are not all inevitable. She wanted to treat her body well, both for her health and also because her body is God's gift which she should care for well. Sandy decided to do what she could to change things. She joined a gym and actually worked out at the gym three times per week. She also became more intentional about what she ate and drank. As the pounds came off and her fitness improved, Sandy found she had more energy, was happier with herself and more patient with others. Two years and 30 pounds later, Sandy had a new outlook on life. She had taken an important step in harmonizing her life by paying attention to her health.

Pursuing Harmony

Life goes well when we pursue harmony. We thrive and our relationships blossom. Rather than living "solo," we seek harmony with others.

Our society often resembles bumper cars. Each person does his own thing and occasionally bumps into someone else or drives alongside another, only to lose touch and move on again. As humans, our problem is we are relational and need to permanently connect with others. Playing bumper cars leaves us dissatisfied and lonely. Harmony happens when we are aware of others and of the different areas of our lives that need attention.

Last summer I participated in a sailboat race in California with some friends. Just like previous times, we hitched the boat trailer to the truck, tossed in our stuff and left red-hot Phoenix for the cool California coastline. We anticipated relaxing recreation and stimulating sailing.

However, this time we neglected something important. As we reached the not-so-exciting town of Quartzsite, Arizona, we quickly checked the trailer's wheels only to discover they were smoking! We further discovered there was little or no grease in the wheel bearings. Without grease, bearings have friction, resulting in heat and smoke. As you can imagine, these were bad things for our trailer wheel and for our sailing plans.

Just like our boat trailer, when you ignore something important, you can have a breakdown. That's why it is important to pay attention to the different area of your life.

Envision your life of harmony as a series of concentric circles.

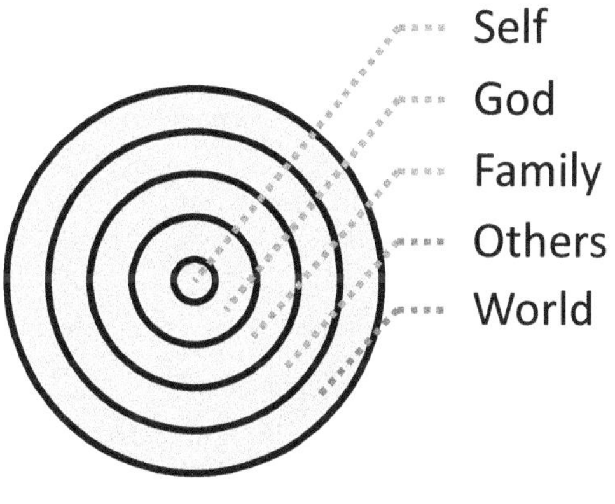

Circles of Harmony

Harmony applies not only to your personal life, but also to your life with God, with your family, with others and with your world.

This may seem overwhelming, knowing that you don't have the luxury of only working on one area at a time. If you focus on only one area of life you may get too much "friction" in another area of life and self-destruct.

Don't get discouraged! As you have worked through this book, you have already made major strides in restoring harmony to your life. You have discovered the old baggage and wounds that caused pain and disharmony. You have identified wrong messages, how they negatively affected you. You have embraced new messages which lead to freedom and joy. You have forgiven people who have hurt you. You have drawn closer to God. You are on your way to personal harmony in life.

Isn't that wonderful to know and to recognize? You are well on your way! With God's help, you will experience lasting life change!

Exercise 13

What change has been most important to you? How has it affected you? How has it affected others? Write it down here:

Now, take a moment and thank God for these changes He has helped you make:

Naturally, these first steps need to be followed by many more. By using the principles and tools from *Keep the Change!*, you will discover new areas for change. This is how we grow as people and become more mature.

Restoring Harmony

Years ago, Barbara and I took 20 college students spelunking (caving) in southern Indiana. I'd never been in a real cave on my own before. I learned three things very quickly:

1. It's dark in there!
2. There is no predicting which way you will go in a cave; there is no rhyme or reason. Sometimes it goes left, sometimes right, sometimes up or down.
3. You need a flashlight!

I needed a flashlight in the cave to see anything. I would shine my light and I could then see far enough ahead to take two or three steps. As I took the steps, my light would show me where the next steps on the path would be.

> *Your word is a lamp to my feet*
> *and a light to my path.*
> *- Psalm 119:105*

In the same way, God's Word provides illumination for us in life. As you listen to Him, you get direction for where you should go and how you should live. Step by step, He will show you how to restore harmony in your life.

As you achieve more harmony in your own life, God wants to also use you in others' lives, to help them live in harmony. Your example, your friendship and your service will make a huge impact on them. Imagine how exciting it will be, to literally see others experience and enjoy the harmony of life that you have discovered!

Life-Changer #13 - Harmonize Your Life

1. Summarize the most important thing you have learned from this chapter:

2. Rate yourself in the following areas of life: (check the box that fits best)

Harmony in Personal Life:

	Great	Fair	Poor	add comments
Health				
Faith				
Character				
Career				
Service to others				

Harmony in Relationships:

	Great	Fair	Poor	add comments
Marriage				
Family				
Extended Family				
Friends				
Neighbors/co-workers				
Other people				

3. Which areas of your life need the most attention, in order to restore harmony? (choose one area from each table)

   In my personal life:

   In my relationships:

4. Where do you need to start? What can you do?

Focus — Read. Reflect. Pray. Do.

Psalm 37:16-18

Better is the little of the righteous than the abundance of many wicked. For the arms of the wicked will be broken, but the LORD sustains the righteous. The LORD knows the days of the blameless, and their inheritance will be forever.

What is the main point of the passage?

How does it apply to me?

My Challenge Today

What challenges / opportunities await me today?

How do I want to respond to them?

My Focus Today

What is my guiding thought for today?

My Prayer Today

Specific things I am trusting God for:

For Further Study this Week

Psalm 119:9-11, Psalm 119:33-40, Psalm 119:57-64,
Psalm 119:97-101, Psalm 119:105-106, Psalm 119:145-150

Final Words

Congratulations, you made it! I trust your journey through *Keep the Change!* has been valuable and life changing. In addition to changing your life, I pray you will be used to positively impact many other people.

When I was in my twenties, I moved to Europe to counsel college students. To be effective, I needed to improve my basic German-language skills to a high level of fluency. In the first three months, I learned a great deal, but I also discovered I had much more to learn. When we left Europe fourteen years later, I was still learning German.

If you've ever learned a foreign language, you know it is an ongoing process. First, you acquire a basic vocabulary and learn some phrases like "Where is the bathroom?" and "How much does this cost?" Then, you expand on this knowledge. You take classes, memorize verbs, talk with native speakers and practice, practice, practice.

There are times when the language learner is frustrated and times when one feels stupid or foolish. You might even be tempted to give up. However, if you persevere, there will also be times when your growing fluency will be richly rewarded.

Doing something that is challenging always seems to take longer and requires more work than you expect. Like learning a language, going through the hard work of changing your life is a challenging task that takes time. It isn't an easy or natural process. It can seem very unnatural, having to overcome the old ways of viewing yourself and the bad habits you learned over the years.

But, life change is worth it. Yes, it takes work. You may discover there is much more to learn and more that needs changing than you originally thought. That is very normal. It is a sign that you are open-minded and are listening to God as He helps you grow and change.

Here are some final suggestions to guide you along the way:

1. *Keep the Change!* Use it as your guide. Review it, take notes, read the scripture verses and pray about the things you have learned.

2. Journal. Invest in a small notebook and write daily about the things you are learning.

3. Listen. You are not alone. Your Creator is with you and wants to help you. Listen to Him speak by reading the Bible. Read the Psalms, the Gospels and then the rest of the Bible. You will be amazed how relevant and personal God's Word is.

4. Friends. Surround yourself with people who share similar values and faith and who also have the goal of growing and changing. Join a Bible study group. Find a good church. Meet a friend for lunch.

5. Serve. From Luke 6:38 we learn:

   Give and it will be given to you. A good measure, pressed down, shaken together and running over, will be poured into your lap. For with the measure you use, it will be measured to you.

   One of the most important ways to keep learning is by giving away what you have already learned. As you reach out to others in love, not only will they be helped, but you will also be blessed.

We Need Your Help!

If you liked *Keep the Change!* ...

- Let us hear from you. Send your feedback to: help@azlifechangers.com.
- Tell your friends about *Keep the Change!*
- Purchase copies for your friends at www.amazon.com
- Purchase the e-book version at www.amazon.com
- Share *Keep the Change!* with your pastor, Bible study or class. Group orders of 10 or more receive a discount, at help@azlifechangers.com
- Visit www.azchristiancounseling.com for up-to-date information about materials, Facebook links, conferences, counseling and more.

www.ingramcontent.com/pod-product-compliance
Lightning Source LLC
Chambersburg PA
CBHW072017040426
42447CB00009B/1655
9780615468815